Jean Rhys

WIDE SARGASSO SEA

Notes by Loreto Todd

MA (BELFAST) MA PII D (LEEDS)

Reader in International English, University of Leeds

LONGMAN
YORK PRESS

YORK PRESS
Immeuble Esseily, Place Riad Solh, Beirut

LONGMAN GROUP LIMITED
Longman House, Burnt Mill,
Harlow, Essex CM20 2JE, England
Associated companies, branches and representatives
throughout the world

First published 1995

ISBN 0-582-23766-1

Phototypeset by Gem Graphics, Trenance, Mawgan Porth, Cornwall
Printed in Singapore

Contents

Part 1

Introduction

The life of Jean Rhys

Biographers have had difficulty in establishing the precise details of Jean Rhys's life. The reasons for this are threefold: first, she lived in obscurity for large parts of her life; secondly, she was never totally at home in Europe, and so she moved from place to place and from country to country; and thirdly, her own life was as eventful and controversial as the life of any fictional heroine. It is, therefore, not always easy to distinguish between Jean Rhys as she was and Jean Rhys as she wanted to be. We can, however, be fairly certain of the following facts.

Her original name was Ella Gwendolen Rees Williams and she was born in Roseau, Dominica, on 24 August, 1890. Her mother, Minna Lockhart Williams, was of Scottish origin and a descendant of slave owners who had lived on the Caribbean island of Dominica for several generations. Her father, William Rees Williams, was a Welsh ship's doctor who met his wife in Dominica. The Williamses were, in many ways, atypical of Dominican society. They were middle-class, Protestant and English-speaking in a community where most people were black, poor, Catholic and creole users. Perhaps the isolation that the family felt may explain the sense of insecurity and alienation that is a predominant theme in Rhys's writings.

In 1907, Jean Rhys left Dominica for England in the company of her father's sister. She was sent to the Perse School for Girls in Cambridge but left at the end of 1908 to enrol in Sir Herbert Beerbohm Tree's School of Dramatic Art in London. It is possible that she would have achieved her ambition to become an actress if she had continued at the college for longer than two terms, but a letter written to her father by the administrator, George Bancroft, suggests that her reasons for leaving were not entirely financial:

> Dear Sir,
>
> In answer to your letter of June 13th [1909] I write to say that your daughter is slow to improve with her accent which in my frank opinion would seriously affect her chances of success in Drama. I fear it would take her a considerable time to overcome this accent which in my judgement would only fit her for certain parts and those perhaps few and far between. (Quoted in Carole Angier, *Jean Rhys: Life and Works*, André Deutsch, 1990, p. 49.)

The next twelve years of her life were lived in obscurity and the only information we have is sketchy. She earned a living for a while as a chorus girl and had an affair or series of affairs and an abortion. She then worked for part of the First World War in a railway canteen in London, and met her future husband, Willem Johan Marie [Jean] Lenglet, in 1917. They were married in The Hague, Holland, in 1919, had a son in 1920 (who died) and a daughter in 1922, and they lived in Paris, Vienna, Budapest and Belgium between 1920 and 1922.

By August 1922 the family was living in Paris, where Jean Lenglet was found to be a bigamist. (He had married a nineteen-year-old Dutch girl in 1910 and, without being divorced, a nineteen-year-old French girl in 1913.) In 1924, he was convicted of currency offences. While he was in prison, Jean Rhys spent a lot of time with the English writer, Ford Madox Ford and his common-law wife, and the evidence available suggests that they set up a *ménage à trois*, while Jean Rhys and Ford began their affair. When Jean Lenglet was released from prison and extradited to Holland, Jean Rhys remained in Paris and began to write. Her first book, *The Left Bank and Other Stories*, was published in 1927, about the time that her liason with Ford ended.

Jean Rhys moved between Paris and London until 1932. In February 1934, after her divorce from Lenglet, she married Leslie Tilden Smith, who ran a literary agency and worked as a reader for London publishers. In 1935, Smith received legacies from a number of estates, which they spent travelling to Dominica and America together.

The biographical evidence of the next period of her life is scant. She developed a serious alcohol problem; her husband died in 1945; and two years later she married his cousin, George Max Hamer. Hamer went to jail for involvement in illegal currency dealing in 1949; and, on his release, the couple lived in abject poverty, first in Cornwall and then in Devon.

During the 1950s, Jean Rhys began to write *Wide Sargasso Sea*, which was published in 1966. It met with such critical acclaim that all her other books were republished and, for the first time in her adult life, she had enough money to live comfortably. She died on 14 May, 1979, the year when her autobiographical book, *Smile Please*, was published.

Rhys's published work

Jean Rhys started writing in her early childhood, but she only considered it as a career when she met Ford Madox Ford in Paris. Her books were:

The Left Bank and Other Stories, 1927
Postures, 1928, published as *Quartet* in New York, in 1929
After Leaving Mr Mackenzie, 1931
Voyage in the Dark, 1934

Good Morning, Midnight, 1939
Wide Sargasso Sea, 1966
Tigers Are Better Looking, 1968
My Day: Three Pieces by Jean Rhys, 1975
Sleep It Off, Lady, 1976
Smile Please: An Unfinished Autobiography, 1979

As well as these, she wrote a number of stories which appeared in magazines, including:

'Vienne', *Transatlantic Review*, Jan. 1925, pp. 639–45
'I Spy a Stranger', *Art and Literature*, winter 1966, pp. 41–53
'Temps Perdi', *Art and Literature*, winter 1967, pp. 121–38
'The Whistling Bird', *New Yorker*, 11 September, 1978, pp. 38–39.

Rhys's Caribbean heritage

Jean Rhys was born on a small, ethnically mixed island in the Caribbean at a time when the population of about 30,000 included approximately 300 whites. The island was visited by Christopher Columbus in 1493 and named Dominica, the Latin word for 'The Lord's Day', because it was first sighted on a Sunday. The French claimed Dominica in the early eighteenth century when they attempted to establish a plantation there. By 1748, their efforts at colonisation had failed, and so the island was declared neutral and left in the possession of its Carib inhabitants and the French settlers who wished to remain. Fifteen years later, in 1763, the British moved to the island with their African slaves. It became a British colony in 1805, although the French influence continued in the widely used French-based creole.

The poet Derek Walcott, who was born on St Lucia, an island on which Jean Rhys spent three months when she was ten, described the feeling, almost of schizophrenia, that was experienced by many people born in the Caribbean at the time of the British Empire. They looked back with nostalgia to their original homeland and yet many of them knew little about it. There was mutual mistrust between many whites and blacks because of the centuries of slavery and yet they understood each other in a way that outsiders could not always comprehend.

Jean Rhys probably experienced similar feelings because, although she was white, few slave-owning families were racially unmixed. She left the Caribbean when she was seventeen and returned only once, for a visit, in 1936, yet Caribbean images of lushness permeate her work and form the background to *Wide Sargasso Sea* which was by far her most successful novel. Her fictional Caribbean world is like a Garden of Eden that has gone to seed. The vegetation is as unregulated as the people. The expatriate society she describes is dying and decadent. The black people are numerically stronger than the whites and threaten the lifestyle once enjoyed by the slave owners. They are, like the creolised languages they use, so similar and yet so different, as if their culture cannot be comprehended by a standardised European language.

The meaning of the term 'creole'

The term 'creole' is, today, used with several different meanings and is therefore liable to be misunderstood. The word derives from the Latin word *criar*, meaning 'to nurse, to breed, to bring up, to nourish'. It was first used in a colonial context in 1590, to mean children 'born of Spaniards' in the New World. In 1609, it could refer both to 'the children of Spaniards by Spanish women' born in Peru and also to 'a Negro born in the Indies'. By 1697, William Dampier, an English adventurer, applied 'Cirole' to 'all born of European parents in the West Indies', but during the eighteenth century, the word appears in English, French and Spanish and could refer to anyone born in the Caribbean. By the early nineteenth century, Lady Nugent, the wife of the Governor of Jamaica, applied the word 'Creole' to language and noted in her diary that 'the Creole language is not confined to the negroes'.

Jean Rhys uses 'Creole' to refer to white people who were born in the West Indies. The de Plana sisters who share Antoinette's school days in the Convent, for example, are Creoles (p. 46). In modern usage, there is a tendency to use a capital 'C' for 'Creole' when it refers to a person or when it is applied to a particular language, such as 'Jamaican Creole'. It is given a lower case 'c' when the term is applied generally to any pidginised language which has become a mother tongue.

Rhys's use of creolised English and French

Dominica, like other islands in the Caribbean, is ethnically mixed, with the majority of the population being of African origin. There, as on all the Caribbean islands, a European tongue was the official language but the majority of the blacks spoke a related form of language, often called a *patois* or a *creole*. Creole languages derive from makeshift communications between people who do not share a mother tongue. Let us examine how the Caribbean varieties came into being.

Contacts between British sailors and coastal West Africans date back to the sixteenth century. Early communication was confined to exchanges involving a limited number of English words, a few simple structures, mostly commands, reinforced by gesture and mime. This type of communication is called a *pidgin* and pidginised forms of Dutch, English, French, Spanish and Portuguese arose as trade languages in Africa as European adventurers traded first in goods and then in people. Pidgin languages are simple and easy to learn because they discard all structural complexities and exploit innate human abilities to communicate.

Pidginised English was used by sailors towards slaves, and the slaves, deprived of any other model, learned and used the pidgin. A clear idea of the linguistic interaction on a slave ship is provided in Barry Unsworth's *Sacred Hunger* (Penguin, 1992). Admittedly, Unsworth's account is fictional but it is based on scholarly evidence.

A creole arises when a pidgin becomes a mother tongue. This happened on a large scale in the plantations established throughout the New World. A chain of related creole Englishes, for example, is found from the Southern States of the USA, through the Caribbean islands and coastal regions of Central America to Guyana and Surinam in South America. Slaves speaking the same African languages were often separated to reduce the risk of plotting and so the only language they shared was the pidginised English they had learnt while in captivity in West Africa, on the long journey between Africa and the Caribbean, or on the plantations. Children born in such circumstances thus learned a form of English as their mother tongue. Creole languages utilise many of the simple structures found in pidgins but they are more flexible and more developed and are capable of fulfilling all the linguistic needs of their speakers. Creoles are in no way inferior to other languages. Indeed, many world languages have undergone creolisation. French, for example, is a creolised form of Latin, and English underwent creolisation after the Norman Conquest in 1066.

Jean Rhys knew Standard English and French but she also had an excellent command of creole English and French. She uses these in her novel to distinguish characters and to evoke a period when racial contrasts were reflected by linguistic differences. In the speech of the black characters, we hear echoes of Africa. Their forms of English and French have often been disparaged, but Rhys knew that they were fully capable of verbalising a culture that had roots in Africa and Europe as well as in the Caribbean.

She does not try to recreate Jamaican Creole in all its subtlety but indicates it by selecting a few features such as:

(1) the use of words of African origin, such as 'obeah' (p. 25), 'jumby' (p. 37) and 'zombie' (p. 42);
(2) the use of sentences without the verb 'to be': 'Old time white people [are] nothing but white nigger now, and black nigger [are] better than white nigger' (p. 21);
(3) the use of adjectives as both adjectives and nouns: '. . . because she pretty like pretty self' (p. 15) (because she is as pretty as prettiness itself) and
(4) the use of verbs without agreement: 'it grow[s] again' (p. 37); 'she creep[s] and crawl[s] like centipede' (p. 85).

The setting for *Wide Sargasso Sea*

Although Jean Rhys draws heavily on her knowledge of Dominica for the imagery in *Wide Sargasso Sea*, the first part of the novel is set in Jamaica. Like Dominica, the island was originally inhabited by Arawak Indians who were overrun and absorbed by Caribs. It was visited by Christopher Columbus in 1494 and colonised by the Spanish in 1509. The Spanish founded sugar plantations in Jamaica and, from 1640, they began to import African slaves to work on them. The island was conquered by the British in 1655 and remained in British hands until independence in 1962. The British continued to bring Africans to Jamaica to work as plantation slaves and the conditions in which they were kept were so inhuman that hundreds of thousands died. In his book, *Revolutionary Empire*, Angus Calder estimated that 'close on half a million slaves' were imported into Jamaica during the period 1700–75 but, because of the high death rate among them, the slave population only rose by 15,000 over this period. The slaves rebelled many times in Jamaica and each rebellion was put down with such brutality that, in England, the call for the emancipation of slaves grew. The Emancipation Act was passed in London in 1833. Slave children were to be freed by 1834 and adults were to work three-quarters of their time for their former owners and use their wages to buy their freedom. The plantation owners no longer needed the labour of their former slaves – the slaves were to be freed and the owners compensated by Britain. However, many freed slaves were left destitute when the work they had done was given to indentured labourers from India.

Wide Sargasso Sea is set in Jamaica shortly after the emancipation of slaves. On the very first page, we are told that Mr Luttrell drowned himself because the promised compensation did not come. We also learn on p. 18 that Christophine had been given as a wedding present to Antoinette's mother. The feelings of unease and uncertainty between blacks and whites is the backdrop against which the first part of the narrative unfolds.

A note on the text

The title of the novel refers to an area of the Atlantic Ocean, known as the Sargasso Sea. This expanse of water is situated between the West Indies and the Azores. It gets its name from the prevalence of sargassum, a floating seaweed, also known as gulfweed. The sea is empty and calm but also stagnant and treacherous and reminds the reader of the gulf between the West Indies and England, between black and white, between Antoinette and Rochester and, ultimately, between good and evil.

Wide Sargasso Sea is available in several editions. For these Notes, all page references will be taken from the Penguin edition (1968), which has an introduction by Francis Wyndham.

Part 2

Summaries
of WIDE SARGASSO SEA

A general summary

Wide Sargasso Sea is written in simple, lucid prose that is both economical and poetic. It tells the story of Antoinette Cosway, the first wife of Edward Rochester who later marries Jane Eyre in Brontë's novel.

Antoinette Cosway was born in Jamaica shortly before the emancipation of slaves in 1834. She is a child when the novel opens and, in Part One, we see people and events through her eyes. She lives with her mother, Annette, her brother, Pierre, and a few freed slaves on a rundown estate called Coulibri. Their standard of living has dropped over the years, partly because of the Emancipation Act, but mostly because Mr Cosway had allowed his estate to deteriorate before he died.

Antoinette's mother marries Mr Mason, a rich Englishman, and as a result their standard of living improves. Annette realises that the former slaves are angry and may attack Coulibri but Mr Mason refuses to take her warnings seriously, with the result that Coulibri is burnt to the ground and Pierre killed. Annette never recovers from Pierre's death and becomes increasingly introverted. Antoinette is sent to a convent school and, for a short time, knows contentment. She is eventually removed from school at seventeen and a marriage is arranged between her and a young Englishman, called Edward Rochester.

At first, they share a strongly physical love, but they know nothing about each other and gradually the lack of knowledge turns to distrust and hate. Rochester is told that there is madness in Antoinette's family and, as he turns against his wife, he thinks he can detect evidence of her instability. Eventually, he decides to take her to England, away from the warmth and the colourful natural beauty that Antoinette has always valued more than people: 'All better than people. Better. Better, better than people' (p. 24).

In England, Antoinette is deprived of freedom, locked in an upstairs room in a cold, country manor and guarded by Grace Poole. Increasingly, she finds that, for her, there is more truth in dreams than in actual events. She accepts hatred and rejection with fatalism: 'I make no effort to save myself; if anyone were to try to save me, I would refuse. This must happen' (p. 50), and waits for the moment when she can win everlasting freedom by her suicide.

Relevance of *Jane Eyre* to *Wide Sargasso Sea*

Charlotte Brontë's *Jane Eyre* was first published in 1847. It is, in essence, a love story between Jane Eyre and Edward Rochester. Rochester's first wife, Bertha, is a Creole from Jamaica and he keeps her locked up in a room without a window. He tells Jane (Chapter 26) that Bertha is mad, that she comes from a family of 'idiots and maniacs through three generations', and that her mother 'was both a mad woman and a drunkard'. Jean Rhys thought that the portrait of Bertha was unjust and *Wide Sargasso Sea* is an attempt to provide Mrs Rochester with a biography that would explain her behaviour. As Rhys explained in the *Paris Review* interview of 1979:

> When I read *Jane Eyre* as a child, I thought, why should she think Creole women are lunatics and all that? What a shame to make Rochester's wife, Bertha, the awful madwoman, and I immediately thought I'd write the story as it might really have been. She seemed such a poor ghost. I thought I'd try to write her a life.

A summary of *Jane Eyre* is provided to explain the background to *Wide Sargasso Sea*.

A summary of *Jane Eyre*

Jane Eyre is orphaned at ten and taken into the home of an aunt by marriage, Mrs Reed. She is unwanted, mistreated and sent to Lowood, a charity school, run by the Rev. Robert Brocklehurst. At first, she and the other children suffer from cold, hunger and the hard, unsanitary conditions, but improvements are made after the death of several children from typhus fever.

Jane stays at Lowood for eight years, six as a pupil and two as a teacher, but decides to leave when the kindly principal, Miss Temple, retires to get married. She applies for the post of governess to Adèle Varens, the ward of a Mr Rochester of Thornfield Hall in the Midlands. For about three months, Jane, Adèle and the housekeeper, Mrs Fairfax, live a quiet, happy life until Mr Rochester comes home. At first, Rochester seems an aloof, frightening figure to Jane but he treats her with kindness and respect. Jane saves his life when his bed catches fire and she realises that she is in love with her employer.

Jane is called to Gateshead where her aunt is dying. Mrs Reed confesses that she had lied to Jane's uncle, John Eyre, who had made a fortune in Madeira. John Eyre had wanted to adopt Jane but Mrs Reed had told him that Jane had died in Lowood. In doing so, she had deprived Jane of the security that her uncle could have provided. After a month at Gateshead, Mrs Reed dies and Jane returns to Thornfield to discover that Mr Rochester is to marry Blanche Ingram.

On Midsummer Night, Rochester tells Jane that he had not really loved

Blanche and he asks her to marry him. Jane accepts the proposal and writes to her uncle in Madeira. A month later, the wedding service is interrupted by a lawyer who produces evidence that Rochester already has a wife, a Creole from Jamaica, called Bertha Antoinette Mason. Rochester tells Jane that he was tricked into marriage fifteen years before and that his wife is irretrievably mad. In an effort to excuse his behaviour, Rochester takes Jane to the attic where Bertha tries to attack him and is then tied to a chair.

Rochester asks Jane to go to France with him as his mistress. She refuses but knows she might weaken if she remains at Thornfield. Jane runs away and finds herself exhausted and destitute in Whitcross, Derbyshire. She is taken in by the Rivers family and receives great kindness from Diana and Mary and from their brother, St John, a clergyman, who helps her find a post as a teacher, earning £30 a year. She tells them that her name is Elliot, but when St John finds out her real identity he also discovers that they are cousins and that she has been left £20,000 by their uncle who had died in Madeira.

Jane insists that they should each have £5000 and the three young women set up house together. St John decides to go to India as a Christian missionary and, although he does not love Jane, he wants her to go with him as his wife. Jane is willing to accompany him as a missionary but not as his wife. St John tries to pressurise Jane into marriage but, as she is weakening, she 'hears' Rochester's voice calling her and asking for her help. She takes a coach to Thornfield and finds that it has been burnt to the ground in a fire started by Bertha Rochester. Bertha died in the fire and Rochester lost his left hand and his sight.

Jane goes immediately to Mr Rochester's other house, Ferndean Manor. Rochester still loves her and needs her more than ever. They are married and find both wordly and spiritual happiness in the union. They have a son and there is hope that Rochester's sight will return.

Detailed Summaries

Part One, pp. 15–25

Part One describes the childhood of Antoinette Mason in her own words.

Antoinette Cosway lives on a dilapidated estate called Coulibri, not far from Spanish Town, Jamaica. She lives with her mother, Annette, a beautiful Creole woman from the island of Martinique, her brother, Pierre, and their servant Christophine. We are not told the precise date but we know it must be 1834 or shortly after that because the slaves have been set free. However, the slave owners have not received the compensation they were promised.

Antoinette is left very much on her own. Her mother devotes most of her time and energy to Pierre who probably suffers from cerebral palsy: Antoinette explains that he 'staggered when he walked and couldn't speak distinctly' (p. 16). She looks to Christophine for love and support. Christophine, like Annette, is from Martinique. She had been a slave and was a wedding present to Annette from Antoinette's father. Neither woman is fully accepted in Jamaica. Christophine is thought to possess supernatural powers and Annette's horse is poisoned, thus putting an end to her only pastime.

Antoinette's childhood is poor and lonely. She has only two dresses and there are just five people whom she knows and trusts well – her mother and Pierre, and the servants Christophine, Godfrey and Sass. Other black people, even children, refer to them as 'white cockroaches'. Seeing how lonely she is Christophine arranges for her to play with a black child, Tia, whose mother is also a newcomer to Jamaica.

The two children meet and swim almost every day. One day, while Antoinette is turning somersaults under water, Tia takes the few pennies that Christopine has given her. They quarrel about the money and Tia goes off wearing Antoinette's dress. Antoinette is forced to go home in Tia's dress to find that her mother is entertaining guests for the first time in years. Christophine feels that the visit is a bad omen: 'Trouble walk into the house this day' (p. 22). That night, Antoinette has a nightmare in which she is being chased by someone who hates her.

After the visit, Annette begins to take a keener interest in life. New dresses are made and Annette is lent a horse so that she can resume her riding. Antoinette no longer has any friends but she finds consolation in nature: 'It's better than people' (p. 24), she thinks to herself.

To the surprise of Jamaican society generally, Annette marries Mr Mason, an extremely wealthy widower 'who could take his pick of all the girls in the West Indies' (p. 24).

NOTES AND GLOSSARY:

when trouble comes close ranks: when people are in difficulty, they often find strength in solidarity

because she pretty like pretty self: because she is as pretty as prettiness itself

Martinique: one of the Windward Islands in the eastern Caribbean. The official language is French and a French creole is also widely used. Annette was a stranger to Jamaica and she was not fully accepted by either the black or the white community

haunted: in superstitious communities, houses are often thought to be haunted when their owner commits suicide

they notice clothes: the reference to the blacks as 'they' so early in the novel indicates the animosity between some blacks and whites in Jamaica at the time. It is, however, less hostile when we see it in context. In Part Two, Rochester criticises Christophine for allowing the hem of her dress to drag on the ground. Antoinette explains that Christophine's behaviour was a sign of her affluence. She had more than one dress and so could afford to get one dirty

marooned: isolated, cut off. It is an interesting choice of word because, in Jamaica, runaway slaves were known as 'maroons'

I too old now: I am now too old. Godfrey, the groom, uses many creole structures. He is a religious man and frequently uses language drawn from the Bible

The devil prince of this world: in St John's Gospel (12:31), Jesus says: 'Now is the judgment of this world; now shall the prince of this world be cast out.' Godfrey suggests in a prophetic way that evil wins, or seems to win, in this life

staggered ... distinctly: Pierre is described as an idiot (p. 25) and Rochester, who never knew him, assumes the truth of Daniel Cosway's claim (p. 82). However, the symptoms described here suggest that Pierre suffered from cerebral palsy and that his condition was not genetic

after that she changed: Annette's depression stems directly from her anxiety about Pierre. Her life changed when the doctor told her, we assume, that Pierre's condition was incurable. Her criticism of Mr Mason is, in part, because he failed to keep his promise to take Pierre to England where 'he would be cured' (p. 31)

shingle: a rectangular tile made of wood and used mainly for roofing

the tree of life: in the Bible (Genesis, 2:16–17), God told Adam that he could eat the fruit from all the trees in the Garden of Eden: 'But of the tree of knowledge of good and evil, thou shalt not eat of it: for in the day that thou eatest thereof thou shalt surely die.' Antoinette suggests that their Jamaican garden was as beautiful and as dangerous as the Garden of Eden and that all the people of Coulibri would suffer the same fate as Adam and Eve: they would be driven out of the Garden because of their sins

green ... white ... purples: Antoinette loves bright colours. She mentions them many times throughout the novel. Rochester, on the other hand, tends to dislike them, preferring browns and whites

glacis: this term is not used in Jamaica but occurs in Dominica and Martinique. Jean Rhys explains that it refers to a covered terrace which runs the length of the house. The word derives from French *glacer*, 'to freeze'. It was used from 1672 to apply first to a slope from a fortification and then to a covered archway which was attached to a house to provide shade. Annette does not like bright light, preferring to walk in her shaded *glacis*

A frown came ... knife: Antoinette's description of her mother is echoed by Rochester on p. 114 when he talks about the frown on Antoinette's face which was 'deep as if it had been cut with a knife'. One of the great achievements of the novel is its ability to suggest a fatalistic inevitability by its use of echoes and repetitions

patois: this term refers to the French Creole of Martinique. Christophine occasionally uses the patois when she tries to console Antoinette in Part Two

à dieu: until [we meet with] God. The single word *Adieu* is the equivalent of 'goodbye forever'

blue-black: French and English slaves often came from different parts of Africa. Those from the Gold Coast area were often darker than those from the Bight of Benin

She was your father's wedding present to me: Christophine was a freed slave. She shows love and loyalty to Annette and her family. As Annette says (p. 19), if Christophine had abandoned them, they would not have been able to survive

let sleeping curs lie: the usual expression is 'Let sleeping dogs lie'. It means that we should not tamper with things that are wrong if they are not causing us any trouble at the moment

These ... left us: there were never many people in Antoinette's life and so she did not find it easy to communicate with others

white cockroaches: a term of abuse for poor whites. Cockroaches are large, brown insects with long antennae. They are household pests and are associated with dirty practices.When Amélie wanted to taunt Antoinette with Rochester's infidelity, she sang a song about a white cockroach (p. 83)

Maillotte: Christophine's friend was also an outsider. Her name is French

Tia: this name means 'aunt' in both Spanish and Portuguese. The term 'titi' is used in several creoles for a little girl

We ate salt fish: Tia taunts Antoinette by suggesting they eat like the poor and cannot even afford fresh fish. According to Tia, Antoinette and her family are 'white niggers' and thus inferior only to the poor blacks

Some people crazy: Christophine suggests that Annette is crazy for not understanding how poor they are. Her ability to speak to Annette this way suggests the intimacy of their relationship

mash up people's feet: to ruin people's feet. 'Mash' deriving from 'smash' is used in many creoles for 'treading on people's feet'

I dreamed: this is the first time that Antoinette has a prophetic dream. She has a second one when Mr Mason first suggests that she will be marrying an Englishman (p. 50). In *Wide Sargasso Sea*, Rhys uses dreams to suggest future events. Charlotte Brontë used dreams in a similar way in *Jane Eyre*. The night before her planned wedding, for example, Jane dreams that she and Rochester are separated and that Thornfield Hall is in ruins (Ch. 25)

sugar works: much of the wealth of the West Indies in the eighteenth century came from its sugar plantations. As the price of sugar dropped in Europe, many of the West Indian sugar refineries ceased to be profitable. They were closed, leaving many slaves 'unemployed' and encouraging slave owners to accept the Emancipation Act

And if ... people: no matter how much plants and animals hurt her, Antoinette finds them preferable to people. She has never known much human warmth except from Christophine

A fantastic marriage: an ill-judged marriage

old Cosway: Antoinette's father, who was not a good provider. Annette, his second wife, was much younger than he and incapable of controlling his drinking or promiscuity

Presents ... Christmas: Mr Cosway and Annette recognised Cosway's illegitimate children and behaved kindly towards them. Antoinette was trained to do the same but

Mr Mason does not approve of her familiarity with her 'coloured relatives'

the boy . . . expression: this is the first suggestion that Antoinette and her brother are both mentally unstable. No evidence is provided for this claim, but this type of whispering affects Antoinette. Even in Thornfield Hall she can hear it: 'So there is still the sound of whispering that I have heard all my life, but these are different voices' (p. 148)

light . . . air: this is probably a reference to Stephen Foster's song 'I dream of Jeannie with the light brown hair/Borne as a vapour on the soft summer air.' Stephen Foster (1826–64) wrote many popular songs including 'The Old Folks at Home' and 'My Old Kentucky Home'. Many of his songs were based on traditional Negro spirituals

---

Part One, pp. 25–38

Annette and Mr Mason go to Trinidad on their honeymoon and Antoinette and Pierre stay with Aunt Cora in Spanish Town while Coulibri is repaired. On returning to Coulibri, they have money and many servants, but their good luck is attributed to Christophine's supernatural powers.

When they have been married for just over a year, Annette senses trouble and tells Mr Mason that they must leave Coulibri. He laughs at her intuition and even a child like Antoinette wants to tell him 'that out here is not at all like English people think it is' (p. 29). Mr Mason thinks that blacks 'are children – they wouldn't hurt a fly' (p. 30) and, in spite of warnings from Aunt Cora, he discusses his plans to import Indian labourers, 'coolies he called them' (p. 30).

One night, Antoinette is told to get up and dress. There is an angry crowd outside the house, but Mr Mason still underestimates the danger from what he calls 'a handful of drunken negroes' (p. 32). They set fire to the back of the house and Annette only just manages to grab Pierre from his burning crib. She screams abuse at Mr Mason, blaming him for their predicament. Aunt Cora takes control and leads them all out of the house. Annette tries to return to rescue her parrot but Mr Mason, now alarmed by the noisy crowd, stops her, and Coco falls to the ground, his clipped wings on fire.

While making their way to the carriage, which Mannie and Sass have prepared, Antoinette sees Tia and her mother and runs towards them. She thinks of living with Tia now that Coulibri is destroyed but Tia throws a stone which cuts Antoinette's face. The two children stare at each other 'blood on my face, tears on hers' (p. 38).

NOTES AND GLOSSARY:

Trinidad: Mr Mason had estates in Trinidad and Antigua as well as in Jamaica

obeah: the practice of supernatural powers for the purpose of hurting someone. The etymology of this word is not certain but it probably derives from the Nigerian Efik word *ubio* meaning a 'charm put into the ground to cause sickness or death', reinforced by a Twi form *o-bay* meaning 'witch, sorcerer'

the Holy Family: Jesus, his mother, Mary, and her husband, Joseph

prayer for a happy death: Christophine is a Catholic whereas most black Jamaicans were Baptists. Many Catholic prayerbooks contain a prayer for a happy and peaceful death. It asks God to preserve us from a sudden death and 'to bring our souls to the glory of heaven after our death'

Nothing alarming ever happened: notice how often words like 'nothing' are used in this novel. They help create an atmosphere of fatalistic determinism

You don't . . . side: Annette criticises Mr Mason's paternalistic attitude to black people, whom he regards as children. She is aware that, like all human beings, they could be good or bad or mixed

Godfrey . . . praying: unlike Christophine, Godfrey is a Protestant who believes that no amount of praying could influence the fate that God has laid out for us from the beginning of time. Myra, the servant who is left in charge of Pierre, shared his beliefs

vexed: annoyed, angered. The word is much more widely used in the West Indies than in Britain

out here . . . think it is: even as a child, Antoinette knew that life in the West Indies was very different from what English people imagined it to be. Equally, her notion of life in England is idealised. (See, for example, the last paragraph on p. 30)

coolies: Asian Indians began to be brought into Jamaica as indentured labourers as early as 1834. They were required to work for a defined period, usually two or three years, for a small, fixed wage which they received only when their contract expired. They were called 'coolies', a term which was, originally, not as derogatory as it is now. The word comes from Hindi *kuli*, meaning 'hire, hired person'. The British used Indian labour in Africa and the Pacific as well as the

Caribbean because they believed that Indians worked hard and rarely complained

her loose hair that had burned: Annette risks her own life to rescue her son and she would have risked it again to rescue her parrot, Coco (p. 35). The theme of burning recurs in the novel: Godfrey and Myra threaten Annette with hellfire; Coco is burnt to death; Pierre dies because of fire; and the novel ends with Antoinette about to set fire to Thornfield

Qui est là?: (*French*) Who is there? Who is it?

Ché Coco: (*patois*) dear Coco (similar to the phrase 'Pretty Polly'). Coco speaks French not English and is one of Annette's links with Martinique. Coco uses the creole rather than the Standard French form of 'dear'. The form could also suggest *Chez Coco*, 'Coco's home'

flambeaux: burning torches. The word is often used for the torches carried in religious processions, thus linking physical and spiritual burning

Myra she witness for us: Myra can verify that everything that happened was an accident

You mash centipede . . . again: if you crush a centipede and leave a little bit unhurt, it will grow complete again

jumby: ghost, person with magical powers. The word is found more widely in Dominica than in Jamaica. It probably derives from the West African word 'njamba', meaning 'god, spirit'

sangoree: sangria, a drink made from wine, sugar, fruit juice and brandy. The word comes from Spanish 'sangaree' meaning 'a bleeding'

Like in a looking glass: Tia and Antoinette were close. Looking at Tia's face was like looking into the future and seeing her own pain

---

Part One, pp. 38–51

Pierre dies on the way from Coulibri; Antoinette is ill for six weeks; and Annette is sent to the country to recover. When Antoinette visits her, she is first embraced and then pushed roughly away. She returns to Spanish Town with Aunt Cora and it is decided that she will go to school in the convent. On her first walk to school, Antoinette is followed by two children who threaten her. She is rescued by her coloured cousin, Sandi Cosway, who treats her with great kindness.

Life in her convent boarding school is an oasis of peace and tranquillity.

She talks to the other girls about clothes and hair styles and about the nuns. When she is seventeen, Mr Mason tells her that she is to leave the convent. He has invited some English friends to Jamaica and suggests that one of them may be interested in Antoinette. She has her nightmare again. Only this time, she is following a man who hates her and she cannot escape. One of the nuns gives her hot chocolate and it reminds her of the chocolate she drank the previous year after her mother's funeral.

NOTES AND GLOSSARY:

a hammock: a stretcher

You didn't know anything: Antoinette knows more than people assume. She has learned to listen and to keep quiet about what she has heard

flung me from her: this is the second time Antoinette is rejected by her mother. The first occasion is described on pp. 16–17 and is also associated with Pierre

Look the crazy girl: Look at the crazy girl. This is the second time that Antoinette is regarded as mad (see p. 25)

sans culottes: (*French*) without pants

zombie: a living person who appears to be dead or a dead body re-animated by a spirit. Zombies are often referred to as the 'living dead'. The word comes from Kongo 'zumba' meaning 'fetish, an inanimate object inhabited by a spirit or containing magical properties'

Sandi Cosway: Antoinette's cousin protects her on this occasion. He is one of the few people who always treats her well

clumsy and swollen: Antoinette is very observant. She notices that the nun's hands seem out of keeping with her position

swearing: complaining. Antoinette would like to have been outside in the 'blue shadow' rather than inside sewing

cross-stitching: an embroidery stitch in which every two stitches form a cross

I will write my name in fire red: as ever, Antointette identifies with bright colours but this is also an ominous foreshadowing of her gruesome death

1839: we do not know how long Antoinette has been at school when she embroiders this date but she was probably not more than fourteen at the time

The Relics: all altar stones had to contain a relic, that is, part of the body of a saint

from the garden of my Spouse: from heaven. A nun is often referred to as the 'spouse of Jesus'

deportment: the way in which a person behaves, physical appear-

ance. Convent schools always took a keen interest in
their pupils' deportment

coiffure: (*French*) hairstyle

without a looking-glass: some nuns advised their pupils not to use
mirrors in order to prevent them from becoming vain.
Nuns were not permitted to use mirrors. This is why
the young Irish nun (p. 46) looked at herself in a
barrel of water

vetiver: (*patois*) a tropical grass. The roots produce an
aromatic oil from which perfume can be made. The
de Plana sisters are associated with French words.
Louise had been born in France

July: we do not know how long Antoinette was at school
in the convent. She was there for at least part of a
year as a daygirl and then for almost two years as a
boarder, while her Aunt Cora was in England

bolt upright: nuns were encouraged not to rest their backs on the
back of a chair

now and at the hour of our death: this is a quotation from the Hail Mary.
The second half of the prayer is: 'Holy Mary, Mother
of God, pray for us sinners now, and at the hour of
our death. Amen.' This section of the novel inter-
sperses thoughts and prayers, linking the peace she
found in the convent with the peace to be found in
death

Let perpetual light shine on them: this is from a prayer for the dead:
'Eternal rest grant unto them and let perpetual light
shine upon them. May they rest in peace. Amen.'

Crucifix: The cross with the figure of Christ on it. Nuns wore a
rosary with an attached crucifix from the belt round
their waists

presumption of despair: Antoinette is remembering words from the
Catholic Catechism. Presumption was defined as 'a
foolish expectation of salvation without making suffi-
cient effort to attain it'. Despair was 'the loss of
confidence in God'. Despair was a mortal sin, that is a
sin for which the punishment might be hell

Lord save me, I perish: these words were used by the disciples (Matthew,
8:25) when there was a storm on the Sea of Galilee.
They awoke Christ and he calmed the sea. Later, in
Chapter 14:25, Christ walked on the water and Peter
tried to do the same. 'But when he saw the wind
boisterous, he was afraid; and beginning to sink, he
cried, saying, Lord, save me.' (30)

over seventeen: this is the first precise piece of information provided on Antoinette's age

One of them will. I'm certain of that: Mr Mason is referring to the fact that one of the people he has invited is to be a suitor for Antoinette

the second time: Antoinette has her dream at times of emotional crisis in her life

She died last year: Antoinette seems to have been at school in the convent for about three years. Her mother died when she was sixteen

---

Part Two, pp. 55–66

Part Two is the longest section of the book. The voice in this part is mainly Rochester's although his name is never actually mentioned. The marriage between Antoinette and Rochester has already taken place. They are on honeymoon in the Windward Islands, on an estate called 'Granbois' (i.e. large wood), which had belonged to Antoinette's mother. The journey from Jamaica seems long and tiresome to Rochester, after his illness and his hasty marriage: 'I was married a month after I arrived in Jamaica and for nearly three weeks of that time I was in bed with fever' (p. 56). Yet, it is Rochester who insists that the wedding go ahead. He has been promised £30,000 as Antoinette's dowry and is disturbed when Antoinette wants to withdraw from the marriage: 'I did not relish going back to England in the role of rejected suitor jilted by this Creole girl' (p. 65). He sets aside Antoinette's worries by promising her trust, 'peace, happiness and safety'.

NOTES AND GLOSSARY:

it was all over: we are not told exactly what 'it' is, but since the second line quotes part of the wedding service 'for better or for worse', we can deduce that Rochester means the engagement and marriage

myself . . . Amélie: it is interesting that Rochester puts himself first. The three people under the tree are the first people we meet in Part Two and, at this stage, they are unaware how closely their destinies are to be linked

lovely little creature: Rochester seems physically attracted to Amélie from the beginning although he thinks of her as a 'creature' rather than as a person

the Windward Islands: a group of islands in the eastern Caribbean which includes Martinique, St Lucia and Dominica

a small estate which had belonged to Antoinette's mother: there is no indication in Part One that Annette owned any property or that the family had ever travelled there on holiday

Caro: in Part One, Antoinette knew a very small circle of people, and she was reticent and withdrawn. Yet, in Part Two, she seems to be friendly with many people on the island

critically: Rochester is aware that he is harsh in his judgment of Antoinette

Creole ... European either: Rochester suggests that his wife may have African blood

debased French patois: Creole French is spoken on the island. Rochester regards it as debased because it is used by former slaves and also because he cannot understand it. He is inclined to despise what he cannot control

so intimate: it seems from this comment that Amélie is aware of Rochester's interest in her

I have fourteen years: this is a direct translation of the French 'J'ai quatorze ans', meaning 'I am fourteen'

A cock crowed: a crowing cock is often used in literature as a symbol of Peter's betrayal of Christ: 'I tell thee, Peter, the cock shall not crow this day before that thou shalt thrice deny that thou knowest me', (the Bible, Luke 22:33). Here it is probably a warning that Rochester will betray Antoinette. There are many religious references in the book

***Bon sirop*:** (*French*) good syrup, a drink containing sugar and fruit juice. Women vendors selling food and drink in the street are found widely in West Africa and the Caribbean

Everything is too much: Rochester is overwhelmed by the size and colour of life on the island. His reaction is to criticise it

Dear Father: readers are given access to Rochester's thoughts in the letters that he composes to his father. Through them we learn that he feels he has been rejected by his father in favour of his 'conceited' elder brother

thirty thousand pounds: this was an enormous sum of money in the nineteenth century. Its value can be estimated when we remember that, in *Jane Eyre*, a legacy of £20,000 was enough to keep four people in comfort for life. The number also echoes the thirty pieces of silver that Judas was paid for betraying Christ (the Bible, Matthew, 26:15)

No provision made for her: the terms of a large dowry normally included financial safeguards for the woman. Antoinette's fate was, however, left entirely in the hands of her husband. This was possibly because Mr Mason died before Rochester arrived in Jamaica and before such arrangements could be made

I have sold my soul: the German legend of Faust who sold his soul to the devil in exchange for knowledge and power is described in Christopher Marlowe's play *Dr Faustus* (first published in 1604)

screw pine: a tall, tropical pine with pineappple-shaped leaves and heavy cone-shaped fruit

it could not last: on first seeing Granbois, Rochester is filled with a sense of foreboding

my da: (*patois*) my nurse. The term indicates closeness and affection

***Doudou, ché cocotte*:** (*patois*) little darling chicken. In Standard French the term *cocotte* is used of a promiscuous woman or prostitute. There is also, possibly, a suggested resemblance between Coco, the parrot who died in the house fire and Antoinette, the cocotte who will meet the same death

unwillingly: Rochester likes to be in control. He does not like following Antoinette. He is both attracted and repelled by Granbois and the islands because these are the places where Antoinette seems dominant

Of nothing, of everything: the word 'nothing' occurs like a refrain in *Wide Sargasso Sea*. Antoinette is content with 'nothing' until Rochester teaches her to hope

press: closet, wardrobe, cupboard

Richard Mason: Antoinette's step-brother. He arranged Antoinette's marriage to Rochester and did not make any legal provision for her. In English law, at the time, everything a woman owned became the property of her husband when she married unless legally binding clauses were added to the marriage contract to guarantee the woman's financial independence. Richard's failure to safeguard Antoinette could have one of three explanations. He may have liked and trusted Rochester whom he felt to be an 'honourable gentleman' (p. 95). Or, he may have felt that, with Antoinette's family history, she was lucky to get Rochester on any terms (p. 95). Or, he may have been angry that his father left 'half his money when he died' (p. 81) to a person for whom he had no obligation to provide

Granbois: Rochester translates this as 'High Woods' rather than 'Great, Large, or Big Woods'. This is not exactly an error but may suggest that Rochester's opinions are to be treated with caution

But I ... a white one: Rochester deliberately played the role of the attentive suitor. Only some of the black onlookers realised that he was behaving hypocritically

She won't marry you: Rochester was not tricked into the marriage. Antoinette's doubts gave him time to reconsider, but he spurned the opportunity and instead doubled his efforts to win her over

promising her peace, happiness, safety: Rochester promised Antoinette not love but peace, happiness and safety, the three qualities she longed for and had possessed, for a short time, in the convent

---

Part Two, pp. 66–82

In Granbois, Antoinette and Rochester are caught up in their passion for each other: 'If I have forgotten caution, she has forgotten silence and coldness' (p. 76). They still know nothing about each other, but for a time they are happy, even though Rochester is aware that he does not love her: 'I was thirsty for her, but that is not love' (p. 78). One morning, one of the servants, Amélie, gives him a letter from Daniel Cosway, who claims to be Antoinette's half brother. He is living on the island and feels cheated because he and Mr Cosway's other illegitimate children are living in poverty whereas Antoinette is rich. He warns Rochester that the Masons have tricked him into marrying a woman about whom he knows nothing, that both her father and mother were mad, and that her brother was an idiot. He claims that Mr Mason was bewitched by her mother and then by Antoinette, to whom he left half his fortune, and that Rochester has been charmed in the same way. Cosway says he has much more information and invites Rochester to visit him.

NOTES AND GLOSSARY:

how beautiful she was: Rochester was certainly attracted to Antoinette, who seemed beautiful to him, at least for a time. Yet again she is closely associated with fire and firey colours (the 'red and gold lights' in her hair) and this serves to increase the sense of inevitability surrounding her death

Coralita: pink flowers the colour of coral

that England is like a dream: Antoinette's ideas of England are based on pictures (see p. 30) and on text books (see p. 92). England is unreal to her. She wants to understand it because of her husband. Rochester finds the islands that she loves strange and 'quite unreal' (p. 67)

Crac-cracs: onomatopoeic word for a Caribbean insect similar to a cricket. The adjective 'cra-cra' is used in some Caribbean creoles to mean 'nervous, erratic'

La belle: the beautiful one

We used . . . August: there was no mention of visits to Granbois in Part One. It is possible that the visits took place after Annette married Mr Mason or even after Coulibri was burnt down. There is no fixed time scheme in the novel. We do not know whether Antoinette married Rochester shortly after leaving school or whether several years had elapsed between Mr Mason's last visit to the school (p. 49) and her marriage. We are never sure what is meant by 'That was after . . .' After she left school? After the death of her brother? or mother? or even after Mr Mason took an unfatherly interest in her (see p. 81)?

She said . . . moon is full: in many cultures, the full moon is associated with madness

bull's blood: strong coffee. Islanders from Martinique, for example, tend to drink strong French coffee, rather than the weaker coffee often preferred in Jamaica. Christophine is also indulging in sexual innuendo. The term 'bull' is sometimes applied to a sexually mature man

They don't care . . . they have: Rochester judges people and their behaviour by English standards. Antoinette tries to show him that customs have to be understood in context

Rose elle a vécu: (*French*) Rose, she has lived. Many poets have used a rose as a symbol for a beautiful woman and many have commented on the transitoriness of life, love and beauty. The quotation is from the French poet, François de Malherbe (1555–1628). Translated, the verse says: 'She was of this world where the most beautiful have the saddest fate. Like a rose, she has lived as long as roses lived, for one morning.'

It was a beautiful . . . nothing: Rochester finds himself responding to the beauty of the island and wanting to understand its mysterious attraction *fer de lance*:   (*patois*) a large venomous snake. The name literally means 'iron (head) of a lance'

Sandi taught me: there was only one reference to her cousin, Sandi, in Part One. He rescued her from the children who taunted her on her way to school (p. 42)

ajoupa: (*patois*) a small shelter

I love it . . . a person: Antoinette's love of place and nature is a constant in her character. She has learned to prefer nature to people (see p. 24)

never without . . . discovered: Antoinette is generous to her coloured relatives. Rochester disapproves of the 'money she handed out so carelessly'. His love of money is commented on by Christophine (p. 94)

Stupid . . . shy: Rochester does not understand local behaviour and tends to criticise what he does not understand

If I have . . . coldness: for a while, love changed both Antoinette and Rochester

I never wished . . . died: Antoinette was happy with her half-life before Rochester taught her to love and to need love. The half-life was merely a time of waiting until death put an end to her existence

Adieu foulard, adieu madras: (*patois*) Goodbye soft, printed silk, goodbye good quality cotton. 'Foulard' and 'madras' were both fine-quality materials. The terms were sometimes applied to both silk and cotton. Christophine had taught Antoinette her patois songs when she was a child (see pp. 17–18). Many of them dealt with a lonely man and a deserted girl. As Rochester says (p. 76), the songs 'haunted' him, almost as if he knew that they would come true

Ma belle ka di maman li: (*patois*) My beautiful one has told her mother (literally 'mother her')

I **wouldn't hug and kiss them:** Rochester keeps black people ('them') at a distance and does not approve of Antoinette's affection for Christophine. In fact, Rochester does 'hug and kiss' Amélie, but in lust, not love

Why did you . . . to me?: Antoinette questions her happiness, knowing that she will lose it

If I could die. Now when I'm happy: many people have thought that it would be best to die at the moment of our greatest happiness. Shakespeare's Othello who murdered his beautiful wife, Desdemona, claims with prophetic irony (II.1): 'If it were now to die, 'twere now to be most happy.' And the Romantic poet, John Keats

(1795–1821), makes a similar point in his 'Ode to a Nightingale':

> Now more than ever seems it rich to die,
> To cease upon the midnight with no pain,
> While thou art pouring forth thy soul abroad
> In such an ecstasy!

Very soon ... as I was: Rochester admits that he was eager for sex and insists that Antoinette soon shared his appetite

Words – less than ... love her: Rochester used words to persuade Antoinette that he loved her, whereas he did not really love her but lusted after her

Nothing that I told her influenced her: Antoinette's ideas about England were not really capable of being changed. They were part of a dream England, composed of pleasant, romantic fantasies

Old Cosway die raving like his father before him: Daniel Cosway claims that Antoinette's father and grandfather had died 'raving'. No-one else appears to support this claim, although there is evidence that her father drank too much and was promiscuous (p. 24)

soon the madness ... come out: Daniel Cosway insists that Annette was mad, like all white Creoles

fini batt'e: (*patois*) that's how it ends, literally 'finished to fight'. Cosway's description of how Annette was expected to end her life is similar to the death described for Bertha, i.e. Antoinette, in *Jane Eyre*

she try to kill her husband: Cosway claims that Annette tried to kill Mr Mason. We have no other evidence of this and it may be a subtle way of suggesting that Antoinette may try to kill Rochester

madness not being all either: Cosway suggests that Annette was promiscuous

But old Mason ... die: Cosway suggests that there may have been some intimacy between Mr Mason and Antoinette

I hear ... kind word for all: Cosway attempts to flatter Rochester. The evidence presented to the reader by Rochester himself does not support the claim that he had a kind word for everyone

three questions: there is a partial truth in each of these questions: Annette was shut away; Pierre was handicapped; Antoinette was inclined to be solitary

nancy: one of the heroes of African and Caribbean folktales is Anancy/Nancy, the spider. He is known for using his intelligence to overcome adversaries who are bigger and stronger. The English expression 'cock-and-bull stories', i.e. tall tales, is the equivalent of Cosway's 'nancy stories'

Amélie: Amélie is used by both Cosway and Rochester to hurt Antoinette

---

Part Two, pp. 82–91

Rochester is disturbed both by the contents of Daniel Cosway's letter and by the fact that everyone – his father and elder brother, Richard Mason, Antoinette and even the servants – knew these things and he did not. He wanders off on his own and is lost in the woods. He is found by Baptiste, whom he tries to question about the abandoned house in the wood and also about zombies. Baptiste refuses to discuss such things and, when Rochester arrives home, he finds that Antoinette's bedroom door is locked.

The narrative voice is taken up once again by Antoinette, who is visiting Christophine in the house left to her by Annette. Antoinette tells Christophine that Rochester no longer loves her and asks for advice. Christophine insists that she should leave him. She is amazed when Antoinette explains that she has no money of her own and is utterly dependent on her husband.

NOTES AND GLOSSARY:

he look like he see zombi: he looks as if he has seen a ghost. Although there is no reason why Rochester should trust the word of an embittered man, he is deeply affected by Cosway's letter

I hit you back white cockroach: Amélie has no respect for Antoinette

She is older ... cruel: Antoinette knows that Amélie will be merciless if she is given the power to hurt her

The white cockroach she buy young man: like Cosway, Amélie suggests that Antoinette has bought Rochester

spunks: guts, courage

I have my house work for me: Annette had clearly looked after Christophine who had been loyal to her when she lived in poverty. In Part One, there is no mention of Annette having a house to give away

sideways: Amélie is rude to Antoinette but frightened of Christophine, who threatens to give her a 'bellyache' that she may not get rid of

a white cockroach ... niggers: Antoinette explains that the descendants of slave owners are criticised by both blacks and whites

when I learned to hide what I felt: Rochester did not like people who showed their emotions. He had learned to hide (and possibly subdue) his emotions when he was very young

my father's ... eyes: Rochester's description of his father and brother are unpleasant. The reader is never certain whether they were really nasty to him or whether he imagined being slighted

paved road ... ruins: throughout the islands there were ruins of formerly prosperous estates

Under the orange ... grass: flowers are sometimes offered to deities. There is a suggestion that the house Rochester found had once belonged to a priest, Father Lilièvre, but that another religion now flourishes

A pavé road: a man-made road. Baptiste is not pleased to find Rochester in such a place and denies that there is a paved road there

You like you catch fever: You look like you have caught a fever. This construction is used in several creoles

zombi: Rochester is fascinated by zombies, the living dead. He helps to turn Antoinette into one

I did not look up: between pages 89 and 98, we hear Antoinette's voice again and, through hers, Christophine's

Mounes Mors: (*patois*) dead people. In many mystic cultures, rocks are associated with the spirits of people who have died

shingled: in Part One, Antoinette felt safe because she kept a shingle beside her bed (pp. 31–2). She associates Christophine with help and safety

beating them against the stones: this method of washing clothes is still used in parts of Africa

he does not love me: Rochester has already told the reader this (p. 78) but Antoinette is now explaining that he no longer makes love to her

hibiscus: a tropical shrub with large white, pink and red flowers. The so-called 'blushing hibiscus' is white in the morning, pink at noon and red by evening

pack up and go: Antoinette asks for advice but does not want to listen to it if it does not suit her purposes. Christophine's advice might even have brought Rochester to his senses if it had been followed

everyone, not only the servants, will laugh at me: Antoinette worries that people will make fun of her and does not listen when Christophine assures her that they are more likely to laugh at Rochester if she leaves him

When man ... man like that: the more you try to make a man love you,
the less you will succeed

All women, all colours, nothing but fools: when it comes to love, all
women, regardless of skin colour, are foolish

look me trouble: who would have believed it!

I have no money: all Antoinette's money has become the property of
her husband

Part Two, pp. 91–8

Christophine's advice remains essentially the same: talk nicely to
Rochester, explain all that has happened, ask for some money and leave.
Antoinette pleads with Christophine to help her regain Rochester's love.
Christophine explains that she might be able to make Rochester return to
Antoinette's bed, but insists that when love disappears there is nothing that
anyone can do. She agrees, however, to help Antoinette on condition that
Antoinette tells her husband the truth about her background and thus put
an end to the worry and fear instilled in him by rumour.

NOTES AND GLOSSARY:

The Mason boy fix it: Christophine suggests that Richard Mason had
deliberately arranged for Antoinette to be completely
dependent on her husband

bad-hearted: cruel, unfeeling

Better not stay in that old house: don't make things worse by staying
in Granbois. Houses, like places, are often thought
to be lucky or unlucky. Christophine suggests that
Granbois is unlucky

too unhappy: Antoinette probably means 'very unhappy'. She uses
a creole structure as she slips into a stream-of-
consciousness description of England

Wolds: chain of chalk hills in north-east England

how I know?: how would I know? How can I be sure?

bam!: a sound suggesting a sudden action which is not
necessarily audible. The word may come from Twi
'bam' with the same meaning

If the man ... love you: if Rochester does not love you, I can do nothing
to help

You can ... or die: Antoinette suggests that Christophine can produce a
potion to make someone love or hate or die. Her
statement is ambiguous. We do not know whether
she would seriously consider killing Rochester or
whether she would kill herself

tim-tim: fairytale, folktale

obeah: African magic
béké: (*Igbo*) white person
doudou: (*patois*) little darling
Bertha: this is the name used for Rochester's wife in *Jane Eyre*
Money have . . . pretty self: everybody likes money but Rochester loves it more than most
doudou ché: (*patois*) dear little darling
Plenty people . . . mother: many people tell unpleasant stories about you and your mother
she turn her face to the wall: she has decided to die
She should be protected, legally: Aunt Cora tries to persuade Richard to safeguard Antoinette's money in the wedding agreement but Richard does not listen
You are trusting him with her life: Richard offers three reasons for not safeguarding Antoinette's finances: Rochester is an honourable man; Richard is not in a position to dictate terms; and Richard would trust Rochester with his life. Aunt Cora makes the point that Richard is, in fact, trusting Rochester with Antoinette's life
The Lord has forsaken us: this recalls Psalm 22 of the Bible: 'My God, my God, why hast thou forsaken me?' It is also a reference to Matthew 28:46
coucriant: (*patois*) wailing ghost, something like a banshee
calabash: the dried, hollowed shell of a gourd, used as a container
asked politely in patois: Christophine's son uses patois as an indication of both courtesy and intimacy
Palm Sunday: the Sunday before Easter. It commemorates Christ's triumphal entry into Jerusalem. In churches, palms are blessed and distributed
a cock crowed: this is the second time a cock crows. See also p. 58

Part Two, pp. 98–113

The narration changes back to Rochester who receives a second letter from Daniel Cosway, threatening to visit Granbois if Rochester does not come to his house. Rochester decides to visit Cosway and is disgusted by the combination of vile and sanctimonious self-pity. He leaves when Cosway tries to blackmail him for £500, but Cosway has the last word by insisting that Rochester is not the first man in Antoinette's life.

When he returns to Granbois, Antoinette tries to tell him the truth about her background and promises to answer any questions he has. In spite of the efforts she makes, he continues to be cold, calling her Bertha even though she dislikes the name. She pours wine for both of them and, even before he drinks it, Rochester longs to bury his face in her hair as he used to do.

NOTES AND GLOSSARY:

I am sorry for you: Amélie's phrase is ambiguous. It could mean that she is sorry he has been trapped into an unfortunate marriage. Later (p. 116), we realise that she feels he will never experience happiness and will, indeed, cause unhappiness for others

Esau: the son of Isaac and Rebecca and twin brother of Jacob. He was tricked out of his birthright (the Bible, Genesis, 25)

he free ... for herself: Antoinette's father was promiscuous but he showed a certain amount of generosity, freeing the slaves he slept with and giving them a piece of land and a hut

I'm always pestering him for money: Daniel Cosway's description of his own behaviour shows what an unattractive person he is

She have ... jail: this is the first indication we have of why Christophine left Jamaica. The information also provides Rochester with the power to threaten Christophine with imprisonment if she does not leave Granbois (pp. 131–2)

She start with Sandi: Daniel Cosway claims that Antoinette has had relationships with men before Rochester, starting with Sandi

you owe me something: Daniel Cosway tries to blackmail Rochester

For a moment ... Amélie: Rochester thinks that Antoinette may have black blood. He is also attracted physically to both Antoinette and Amélie

Not long ago: this statement suggests that Antoinette married Rochester shortly after she left school. Her mother died when she was about sixteen (p. 51)

She did die ... know about: part of Antoinette's mother did die when she discovered that Pierre's problem was incurable (p. 16)

'Two at least,' I said, 'for the fortunate': Rochester's comment is like a prophesy. Antoinette will die many times before her life is finally ended

I loved it ... so often: Antoinette had given her love to places until she met Rochester. Here she compares the indifference of those places to that of Rochester's God

For five . . . to live: Antoinette and her family had been very poor for five years and that can seem like an eternity

Disastrous: in Part One, Sass had stayed loyal to the family for a while. It is only at this stage of the novel that we learn his full name

I saw the man . . . kiss her: Annette was left to the mercy of a man who could use her as he chose. Christophine explains later that the man who was in charge of her 'take her whenever he want'. In view of such cruelty, it is not surprising that Annette drank

Bertha: Antoinette dislikes the name, but Rochester insists on using it. He had found out that it was one of Annette's names (p. 94)

but I swear . . . used to do: Rochester accuses Antoinette of tricking him into love-making by putting a love potion into his wine, but here he admits that he wanted to make love to her before he touched the wine

---

Part Two, pp. 113–33

When Rochester wakes up, he is violently sick and is convinced that he has been poisoned by one of Christophine's potions. Next night, Rochester makes love to Amélie, knowing that there is only a thin partition between the room they are in and Antoinette's bedroom. The following morning, he gives Amélie some money and sends her away. Antoinette has gone to see Christophine but comes back after three days. Christophine pleads with Rochester to forget all that has happened and to love Antoinette again. When he refuses, she entreats him to give Antoinette some money and to leave his wife in her care. Rochester refuses this as well and forces Christophine to leave by threatening to have her arrested for trying to poison him.

NOTES AND GLOSSARY:

I have been poisoned: the love potion seems to have made Rochester very sick although his wandering in the forest may have been responsible. On p. 88 Baptiste warned him about catching a fever

I looked at . . . knife: this description of Antoinette is very similar to the description of Annette on p. 17

Her torn shift: Rochester is rough in his love-making, a point stressed by Christophine on p. 124

she had drained hers: Antoinette was not hurt by the potion, even though she had drunk it all. It is, perhaps, ironical that its effect was not greater on Antoinette. As Christophine told Rochester: 'She love you so much. She thirsty for you' (p. 129)

I had not ... bedroom: Rochester deliberately used Amélie to pay Antoinette back for 'poisoning' him. He knew that she could hear what he and Amélie were doing and he felt no guilt or regret

I told her ... present: Rochester treated Amélie like a prostitute, paying her off the next morning. Amélie, however, has also used him to further her plans to go to Rio. She could also feel a sense of superiority in that she had only sold her body whereas he had lost pride and dignity and compassion. At this moment, too, Amélie could feel sorry for Antoinette, who had not as much freedom or independence as a servant girl

I noticed that he did not call me 'sir' or 'master': the servants did not approve of Rochester's behaviour. The cook would not stay in the same house and Rochester forfeited the right to any title of respect

Mr Fraser: a retired magistrate (see p. 64). During the three days that Antoinette was away, Rochester plotted to punish Christophine

Pheena: Rochester uses Antoinette's pet-name for Christophine (e.g. p. 120), aware that he now has the power to separate Antoinette from a stong ally

Que komesse!: (*patois*) What is happening? What's wrong?

You abused ... difference: Antoinette points out that Rochester had behaved exactly like the planters he criticised, using a girl and then paying her off

You are trying ... name: Antoinette realises that Rochester's use of Bertha is another method of imposing his will on her

It's not the girl: Antoinette can forgive Rochester's infidelity. What she finds hard to forgive is his wanton destruction of her peace and happiness. He has even destroyed the memories of earlier happiness

Benky: crooked, bandy

Charlie over the water: the Stuart Pretender to the English throne. When James II was deposed in 1688, his son, Charles, had a claim to the English throne. Many people, especially Scots, who were loyal to the Stuarts drank a toast to 'Charlie over the water' i.e. Charles living in France

Why you do that: Christophine stands up to Rochester, asking him why he had not the courtesy to take Amélie somewhere else

Ma belle ka di: (*patois*) My beautiful one has said
marionette: a puppet doll whose limbs can be controlled by strings
Ti moun: (*patois*) Little person, little one
Doudou ché: (*patois*) Dearest darling
Do do l'enfant do: (*patois*) Sleep child sleep
Nobody is to have any pride but you: Rochester assumes that Antoinette has told Christophine everything but, in fact, Antoinette is too proud to tell all that happened. Christophine found out a lot by observation and questioning
you pay for it one day: Christophine threatens that Rochester will suffer for his cruelty to Antoinette
machete: cutlass, large sharp knife used to cut sugarcane
Rupert the Rine: Prince Rupert of the Rhine (1619–82) was the German nephew of Charles I. He was for the Royalist cause during the Civil War and was commander of the Royalist fleet between 1648 and 1650. After the Restoration of the Stuarts to the English throne (1660), he became Admiral of the Fleet and a number of ports are called after him
You make ... at her: You made her think you were madly in love with her. Rochester silently acknowledges the truth of Christophine's claim. Later (p. 127), he admits to himself that he intended Antoinette to hear his love-making with Amélie
But she hold out: Rochester has tried to subdue Antoinette but she is stronger than he realises
swear like half past midnight: swear like a trooper. By half-past midnight a drinker would have consumed enough alcohol to have lost all inhibitions and so would have sworn without reservation
She will never ... die first: Antoinette loves Rochester passionately but will never again ask for his love
He is no Cosway either: Christophine claims that Daniel is not related to Antoinette, a claim reinforced by Daniel (p. 102) and Amélie (p. 99)
That man ... he want: Christophine suggests that Annette's 'madness' was comprehensible in view of the life she was forced to lead. The man who was supposed to look after her raped her whenever he felt like it
oh yes I did: Rochester admits to himself that Christophine is right and that he did love Antoinette
Read and write I don't know: when Rochester blackmailed Christophine

into leaving Antoinette, he told her she could write. Christophine was illiterate but mentioned that she had other knowledge and skills. Later, in Part Three, when Antoinette called on Christophine for help, 'looking behind me I saw that I had been helped' (p. 154)

Part Two, pp. 133–42

Rochester decides to leave Granbois and return to Jamaica. He notices the terrible changes that his behaviour has provoked in Antoinette. On the day of their departure, he weakens for a moment, 'certain that everything I had imagined to be truth was false' (p. 138), but the moment of tenderness passes.

NOTES AND GLOSSARY:

le bon Dieu: (*French*) the good God

dormi: (*French*) sleep

I divided ... woman: even before they left the West Indies, Rochester had envisaged the third-floor room where Antoinette was to be held in Thornfield Hall

oleanders: poisonous evergreen tree

Pity ... the blast: this line is a quotation from *Macbeth*, Act I, Scene 7, lines 21–2

morne: the patois word used for mountain also means 'sad', 'lonely'

everything I had imagined to be truth was false: for a while, Rochester thought that he was wrong to believe all that he had heard against Antoinette. For a short while, he was on the verge of accepting love even when he did not understand it

solitaire: a song bird. The name echoes Rochester's sense of solitariness

paltry money: Rochester is not being honest here. £30,000 was then a great deal of money

He asked me ... we left: Antoinette speaks only once to explain why the young boy is crying. He loved Rochester and wanted to go with him. Antoinette had promised that he could, but Rochester rebukes her, telling her she had no right to make promises on his behalf

wept like Magdalene: Mary Magdalene was cured of evil spirits in St Luke's Gospel (8:2). In Christian tradition, she was thought to have been a prostitute who wept copiously for her sins

I had meant to give it back to her: Rochester had thought of giving Granbois back to Antoinette, just as he had thought of making legal provision for her (p. 59). Neither good intention was fulfilled

---

Part Three, pp. 145–155

Part Three is the shortest section of the book. In it, we hear the voices of Antoinette and Grace Poole, the woman whom Rochester hires to guard her in England. Antoinette lives in almost total isolation, locked in a room with only one window, which is too high to see through. It is cold and damp. She has no mirror and her mind wanders from past to future, from dream to reality. She does not always remember what she had done, but Grace Poole explains that she was tied up because she attacked Richard Mason when he visited.

Antoinette has a dream in which she takes Grace Poole's keys when she is sleeping, goes downstairs silently, lights all the candles, causes a fire, rushes upstairs on to the battlements and jumps to freedom. Antoinette waits until Grace Poole is asleep. She now knows what she has to do.

NOTES AND GLOSSARY:

His stay ... knowledge: Rochester's housekeeper, Mrs Fairfax (Mrs Eff), liked her employer when he was young and thinks that his stay in the West Indies was responsible for changing his character. She sides with Rochester and has no sympathy with anyone who helped to change him

that girl who lives in her own darkness: the young woman who lives in a world of her own

flames shoot up and they are beautiful: fire reminds Antoinette of the warmth, light and colour of her home

the drink without colour in the bottle: gin. Antoinette knew rum, brandy and wine but not gin

Was it that ... food?: Antoinette had tried to escape by appealing to one of the stewards who brought food to her cabin

my wrists were red and swollen: in Chapter 20 of *Jane Eyre*, Richard Mason is taken to see 'Bertha'. She injures him with a knife and is tied to a chair by Rochester

I saw a girl coming out of her bedroom: the girl is Jane Eyre, who becomes Rochester's second wife

red dress: in Chapter 36 of *Jane Eyre*, Rochester says that 'Bertha' was wearing a red dress when she set fire to Thornfield and jumped off the battlements. Antoinette wants it because she was wearing a red dress the last time she saw Sandi

Why they ... understand: Grace Poole cannot understand why such rich people give her such poor clothes to wear

That was the third time I had my dream: Antoinette's dream echoes the description of what happened in *Jane Eyre*

I did not ... haunts this place: this is an unexpected touch of humour. Antoinette has heard of the ghost that haunts the house (p. 149) and does not want to meet it

Aunt Cora's room: Antoinette 'dreams' about people from her childhood, Aunt Cora, Christophine and Tia

I had been helped: Christophine was with her in spirit

shouting: Rochester tells Jane Eyre that he had shouted and tried to rescue 'Bertha'

all my life was in it: drowning people are supposed to see their lives flash by before they die. Antoinette saw her life in the sky. Red is the colour of martyrdom

Commentary

Background

Wide Sargasso Sea was Jean Rhys's last novel. It is based on Charlotte Brontë's novel *Jane Eyre* in the sense that it takes two of its characters, Rochester and his wife, and writes about their meeting, their marriage and their subsequent disenchantment with each other. In an interview in the *Paris Review* in 1979 (see p. 12), Jean Rhys makes clear that the plan for the novel had developed over a long time. The writing took almost as long. Each character was evaluated and every situation scrutinised, with the result that the novel has a structural integrity more frequently found in poetry than in prose.

Jean Rhys took a literary risk in writing a prelude to one of the most widely read novels in the English language. *Wide Sargasso Sea* could have been seen as merely derivative or dependent. Her gamble, however, paid off. It is perhaps the consummate compliment that one can pay *Wide Sargasso Sea* to say that, far from being a mere appendage to *Jane Eyre*, it is a novel of power and sensitivity in its own right as well as being a work which encourages the reader to reconsider *Jane Eyre*. But it does much more even than that. It makes us ask questions about aspects of life, such as madness, for example. What is madness? Is it the result of nature or nurture? Is it an escape when conditions become too hard to bear? The novel also makes us ask questions about human relations. Is there always a struggle for dominance in a sexual relationship? Is dominance more important to some men than happiness? Can any relationship be destroyed by gossip? And it makes us ask questions about slavery. Were the slave owners any worse than the 'entrepreneurs' who criticised them but made more money out of the West Indies? Were black people the only ones who could be bought and sold?

Each reader will attempt to answer such questions in their own way and their answers are likely to be tentative, leading them to question their own assumptions. It is a mark of the greatness of *Wide Sargasso Sea* that it will haunt the reader. We will never know for sure whether Antoinette was utterly innocent or worldly wise, whether Rochester was callous and calculating, or a young man caught up in events that he was powerless to understand, let alone to control. Jean Rhys places the evidence before us and each of us must judge for ourselves.

Structure

Wide Sargasso Sea is divided, not into chapters, but into three parts, each of which is written as if in a different voice. (A similar technique was used by Emily Brontë in *Wuthering Heights*.) The voice in the first part is that of Antoinette Cosway, the name given by Rhys to the first Mrs Rochester. It is the voice of a young Creole girl living in Jamaica shortly after the Emancipation Act of 1833. She, her brother and her mother live in poverty, surrounded by the trappings of the wealth of earlier days. The mother, who loses her estates, her son and then finally her mind, lives in isolation in the country, at the mercy of her carers. The section ends when Antoinette is seventeen and is being withdrawn from school to be married.

The voice in the second part is almost exclusively Edward Rochester's, although we do not know this for certain until Part Three and we are never, in fact, given his name. He describes the early days of their marriage and the widening gulf created by their different backgrounds, aspirations and expectations. Towards the end of Part Two, Antoinette's voice is heard. She is making a final effort to keep her husband's love and, perhaps because she knows her task is hopeless, the visit to Christophine is etched into her memory:

> I can remember every second of that morning, if I shut my eyes I can see the deep blue colour of the sky and the mango leaves, the pink and red hibiscus, the yellow handkerchief she wore round her head, tied in the Martinique fashion with the sharp points in front, but now I see everything still, fixed for ever like the colours in a stained-glass window. Only the clouds move (pp. 97–8).

Shortly after this, Rochester's voice resumes the narrative and, to begin with, it sounds very much like Antoinette's:

> I sat on the veranda with my back to the sea and it was as if I had done it all my life . . . I knew the shape of the mountains as well as I knew the shape of the two brown jugs filled with white sweet-scented flowers on the wooden table. I knew that the girl would be wearing a white dress. Brown and white she would be, her curls, her white girl's hair she called it, half covered with a red handkerchief, her feet bare (p. 98).

We notice two differences, however. Antoinette opens herself to the sensual beauty of nature; Rochester turns his back to the sea; Antoinette sees the island in all its technicoloured glory; Rochester's vision is almost entirely in monochrome, brown and white with only a touch of red. Part Two ends with their preparation to return to England. Their short period of closeness is over.

The voices in the third part are those of Grace Poole and Antoinette, who is now assumed to be mad, although her madness may simply be a form of escape from intolerable loneliness. She has a dream in which she sees her escape by means of death in the fire at Thornfield Hall. This section and the novel end as she goes to put her dream into effect.

The structure of *Wide Sargasso Sea* can be represented as shown in this diagram.

WIDE SARGASSO SEA

Part One	Part Two		Part Three
Antoinette	Rochester	Antoinette	Rochester	Grace Poole	Antoinette

Antoinette's voice is in control in Parts One and Three and takes up about one eighth of the narrative in Part Two. Almost 60 per cent of the novel's narrative is given to Rochester. The voices of all the other characters, with the exception of Grace Poole, are filtered through Antoinette and Rochester.

In choosing to create a narrative that is composed entirely of the voices of her characters, Jean Rhys produces a novel which has more in common with a Shakespearean play than with more traditional novels. In a Shakespearean play, for example, the audience is not provided with precise information about the age, background and experience of the characters. We hear what is said; we see what is done; and we draw our own conclusions. In *Wide Sargasso Sea*, we know what the main characters say and think; we know what they do and we have some idea why they do it; but we are never certain that we are in possession of all the facts. In novels such as Jane Austen's *Emma*, there is an omniscient narrator who may sympathise with individual characters but who is separate from them. Emma may make mistakes, but the narrative voice establishes truths that readers can depend on. We have no such 'truths' in *Wide Sargasso Sea*. We only have aspects of the truth. The result of this technique is that we are not able to pigeon-hole characters. Like real people, they change, develop, grow and are capable of surprising us, just when we think we understand them.

We identify closely with the characters because we hear their words, listen to their thoughts, and share in their pain. Jean Rhys's narrative style can, in part, be comprehended by the term 'stream of consciousness', a term that refers to a representation of a continuous and unexpurgated flow of thoughts and sensations. The term is modern, first coined by William James in 1890, but the techniques associated with it are not exclusively contemporary. They can be found, not only in modern novels, but in Shakespearean soliloquies and interior monologues, in which the mental processes of a character are revealed. The techniques involved in stream of consciousness include:

(1) the use of short, often verbless sentences;
(2) the use of unanswered questions;
(3) the use of unfinished sentences;
(4) the use of repetitions of word and structure;
(5) rapid shifts in subject matter;
(6) links established by association rather than logic.

A good example of Jean Rhys's use of stream of consciousness is provided on p. 92:

> England, rosy pink in the geography book map, but on the page opposite the words are closely crowded, heavy looking. Exports, coal, iron, wool. Then Imports and Character of Inhabitants. Names, Essex, Chelmsford on the Chelmer. The Yorkshire and Lincolnshire wolds. Wolds? Does that mean hills? How high? Half the height of ours, or not even that? Cool green leaves in the short cool summer. Summer.

Characters

The main characters in *Wide Sargasso Sea* are Antoinette, Rochester and Christophine. Their fluctuating relationships symbolise the unbridgeable gulf between Jamaica and England, between Antoinette and Rochester. It is a calm sea on which seaweed grows so profusely that it can almost appear to be land. Like their relationship, it is stagnant and unproductive, a metaphor of their incompatibility. Antoinette shares a fundamental understanding with Christophine that is always missing in her relationship with her husband. She loves the West Indies, its warmth and colour, and cannot think of England as anything more than a dream. Rochester is, for a time, infatuated with both Antoinette and the Caribbean, but he breaks away from both. In response to Antoinette's question 'Is it true . . . that England is like a dream?' his thought is 'No, this is unreal and like a dream,' (p. 67).

Antoinette Mason (née Cosway)

Antoinette shares a first name with Marie Antoinette, the doomed wife of Louis XVI. Her surname 'Cosway' is almost a causeway, a link that is not quite established. Her first name also overlaps her mother's, indicating, perhaps, that their fates were linked, that the daughter would not be able to learn from her mother's mistakes, that Annette's history would be repeated in Antoinette's. Jean Rhys changed the name of Charlotte Brontë's 'mad Creole woman' from Bertha to Antoinette and the change is significant for several reasons. Firstly, whereas 'Bertha' is English, 'Antoinette' is French, reinforcing the gulf between husband and wife. Secondly, 'Antoinette' is also a diminutive and there is, indeed, a childlike quality about the heroine. She responds emotionally to places and people, and turns to Christophine, a mother figure, in her moments of crisis. Finally in Chapter 26 of *Jane Eyre*, it is revealed that Rochester is married to Bertha Antoinetta Mason. Selecting 'Antoinette' allowed Jean Rhys to describe her heroine's potential before she had been turned into Rochester's 'mad woman'.

Antoinette is as much a child of Jamaica's lush landscape as Cathy and Heathcliff are children of the moors in *Wuthering Heights*. She tells Rochester: 'I love it more than anywhere in the world. As if it were a person. More than a person' (p. 74). To take her away from this love was to deracinate her, causing her to lose her home, her orientation, her friend, Christophine, and even her mind. She is an extremist, willing to reject Rochester's marriage proposal (p. 65), but capable of passionate devotion to him. As Christophine tells him: 'She love you so much. She thirsty for you' (p. 129).

Antoinette is rejected by all the people she allows herself to love, except Christophine. She is rejected twice by her mother, once as a child when Annette realises that Pierre's illness is incurable (p. 17) and again after Pierre dies (p. 40). In spite of these rejections, she loves her mother. As a child, she tries to smooth away the frown on Annette's brow (p. 17). As a young girl, she rides out alone to rescue her mother, determined 'to kill anyone who is hurting my mother' (p. 110), but she runs away in horror when she realises that Annette is no longer capable of being saved. She is also rejected by Tia. When Coulibri burns, she runs away to Tia, the little girl with whom she had played, eaten and slept. 'I saw the jagged stone in her hand but I did not see her throw it' (p. 38). The children have been forced into different camps: 'We stared at each other, blood on my face, tears on hers' (p. 38). And finally, Antoinette is rejected by Rochester. She learns to love him, only to be discarded. He allows himself to be persuaded by lies and half-truths; he abuses her by making love to Amélie in the room next to hers.

Antoinette is affectionate and generous. Rochester notices how she hugs and kisses the local people (p. 57), how she gives money away 'carelessly, not counting it' (p. 75) and that visitors never left without 'a large meal and a shot of rum' (p. 75). Even when she has given up her struggle to keep Rochester's love, she puts aside her own troubles to explain why the young boy is crying (p. 140) and to persuade Rochester to take the boy with them (p. 141).

Antoinette has pride. She reveals some of her problems to Christophine because she has no-one else to turn to, but she keeps many things to herself (p. 124), too proud to disclose them to anyone. She also has courage. This is demonstrated when she fights Rochester's attempt to subject her will to his. As Christophine puts it: 'But she hold out eh? She hold out' (p. 126). It may seem strange to a modern readership that

Antoinette did not take Christophine's advice: 'A man don't treat you good, pick up your skirt and walk out' (p. 91) but, in the nineteenth century, a wife was subject to her husband. Without money, she was utterly dependent on him and, even if she had run away with Sandi, he could have forced her to return to the home he provided.

Her dream which foretells her escape is an act of identification with her past. The flames are red like her red dress and warm like her island sun. Her behaviour is, in part, an act of vengeance but it is primarily an attempt to be free. She may die when she leaps but, like Coco the parrot in Part One, it is a price she must pay in order to be released from her cage. It is possible to interpret aspects of Antoinette's character in a different way. Daniel Cosway suggests that 'old Mason take a great fancy for the girl Antoinetta' (p. 81), that she 'know Sandi since long time' (p. 103), that she has led an immoral life 'and she hardly more than a child' (p. 103) and that Rochester was 'not the first to kiss her pretty face' (p. 104). We have virtually no evidence to support any of these claims. It is true that Mr Mason left her half his fortune, but would he have done this for a mistress? It is also true that Antoinette and Sandi had 'often kissed before but not like this' (p. 152), that is, the way they kissed when they said goodbye. Jean Rhys does not tell us exactly how we should evaluate Antoinette. She provides her readers with pieces of information, allowing them to draw their own conclusions.

Edward Fairfax Rochester

Rochester is never mentioned by name in *Wide Sargasso Sea* but his character is clearly developed by means of his own words in Part Two, and through those of Antoinette, Christophine, Grace Poole and Mrs Fairfax. The novel refers to him only as an 'English friend' (p. 49), 'he', 'Sir' (p. 79), 'my husband' (p. 91) and 'Master' (p. 117). In not giving him a name, Jean Rhys distances him from the reader. Without a name, he remains less than human, mysterious and threatening. (You might like to consider whether, indeed, we weaken the impact of his character by using the name provided in *Jane Eyre*.)

Rochester is calculating and determined to make money. At the time, an easy way to do this was to marry an heiress, and he travels to Jamaica specifically to do so. He is distressed when Antoinette calls off the wedding, but only because his pride and his prospects are hurt: 'I did not relish going back to England in the role of rejected suitor jilted by this Creole girl' (p. 65). He sets out to make her change her mind, kissing her 'fervently' (p. 66) and promising her 'peace, happiness, safety', three of the qualities Antoinette longed for. Rochester is not criticised for being interested in money. As Christophine says: 'Money have pretty face for everybody' (p. 94). He is criticised for being interested in money to the exclusion of everything else: 'Your husband certainly love money ... for that man money pretty like pretty self, he can't see nothing else' (p. 94).

His premeditated cruelty is shown in his dealings with Antoinette and with three other characters. He makes love to Amélie to hurt Antoinette and then pays her off as if she were a prostitute (p. 116); he forces Christophine to leave Antoinette by threatening to have her put in jail (pp. 131–2); and he shows total indifference to the young boy who loves him and who wants to go to Jamaica with them, regarding him as a 'stupid boy' (p. 142) for crying so much.

Yet Rochester's behaviour is comprehensible. He is a younger son and feels rejected by his father in favour of his elder brother. His basic instincts are reasonable. He knows that he should safeguard Antoinette's financial position (p. 59); he intends to give her Granbois (p. 142); he recognises the truth of Christophine's criticisms (p. 127); and he realises that in destroying Antoinette, he is also destroying himself: 'She had left me thirsty and all my life would be thirst and longing for what I had lost ...' (p. 141).

His cruelty is, in part, a reaction to his insecurity, and Daniel Cosway plays on this insecurity. He is reminded that he knows nothing about Antoinette, or about her mother or father, and that Jamaica is very different from England. The worlds they represent are mutually exclusive. Antoinette asks if it is true 'that England is like a dream?' (p. 67) and Rochester insists: 'No, this is unreal and like a dream.' Rochester feels alone and alienated. Indeed, 'alien' is frequently used: 'It was a beautiful place ... with an alien, disturbing, secret loveliness' (p. 73).

Rochester's feelings for Antoinette and the West Indies go through a series of changes. When he arrives, he is indifferent to both people and place. As his infatuation with Antoinette grows, he becomes aware of the magic and charm of the island (p. 73). Fear that his wife may have lied to him leads to hatred of both her and the places Antoinette loves:

> I hated the mountains and the hills, the rivers and the rain. I hated the sunsets of whatever colour, I hated its beauty and its magic and the secret I would never know. I hated its indifference and the cruelty which was part of its loveliness. Above all I hated her. For she belonged to the magic and the loveliness (p. 141).

Rochester is like Shakespeare's Othello. He does not understand the character or the actions of the woman he marries. He is drawn to her beauty and to her sense of mystery, but he is suspicious and afraid. Given the circumstances, tragedy is, perhaps, inevitable.

Christophine Dubois

Christophine, whose name is a blend of Christine and Josephine, does not control a narrative, but her voice comes through very strongly in both

Parts One and Two. She was a slave, and was originally given as a wedding present to Annette by Mr Cosway and, like Annette, she was from Martinique and because of this was always treated with suspicion by the Jamaicans.

Christophine remains loyal to Annette even when she is set free. She stays with the Cosways in their poverty and, as Annette says (p. 19), if Christophine had abandoned them, they would not have survived. In return for such loyalty, Annette gives Christophine a house (p. 84), ensuring her independence.

Christophine is feared because of her obeah powers and we learn from both Daniel Cosway (p. 103) and Mr Fraser (p. 118) that she has been put in jail because of them. Christophine acknowledges that she can make love potions (p. 97) and give someone a bellyache (p. 84), but she knows that if Rochester has stopped loving Antoinette, her 'medicine' will not change the situation (p. 93). She understands the power of the human mind and tells Rochester that he is working his own obeah in calling Antoinette 'Bertha'.

Christophine loves Antoinette and is really the only mother Antoinette knows. In Part One, she notices the child's loneliness and introduces her to another child, Tia (p. 20). She sings patois songs to her (pp. 17–18) and helps her to cope with her fear of the dark. In Part Two, she gives Antoinette good, practical advice: 'A man don't treat you good, pick up your skirt and walk out' (p. 91), but she allows herself to be persuaded by Antoinette, on condition that Antoinette tells Rochester the truth about her mother and brother (p. 96). Later, when Rochester sleeps with Amélie, Christophine stands up to him and fights for Antoinette. First, she tries to put things right between them. When that proves impossible, she asks Rochester to treat Antoinette generously and give her enough money to live on. Rochester forces her to leave Antoinette by threatening to have her put in jail. Even then, she leaves with dignity and promises that, although she cannot read and write, she will keep in touch with Antoinette by other means (p. 133).

Christophine is a pragmatist, not given to daydreams or to idle speculation. She is strong and practical, knowing both when to fight and when to acknowledge defeat. In some ways, she might be described as a 'liberated woman'. Released from slavery, she had no intention of enslaving herself to a husband: 'Three children I have ... each one a different father, but no husband, I thank my God. I keep my money. I don't give it to no worthless man' (p. 91). Her opinion of men is not high, but her opinion of women is equally clear: 'All women, all colours, nothing but fools' (p. 91).

Christophine is strong, loving and loyal. She has learnt to expect very little from life or from people and, like all the characters in the novel, this is exactly what she gets.

Annette Cosway/Mason

Annette's voice is never clearly heard but her actions affect all the other characters. She is married, very young, to Antoinette's father and left in poverty in Jamaica with two small children. With Christophine's help, she manages to survive, but her personality changes when she discovers that her son's condition is permanent. She rejects Antoinette and lives in the shade in her *glacis* until Mr Mason offers her marriage and security. There is a strong suggestion that part of her reason for marrying again was to try to save Pierre. Mr Mason had promised to take him to see doctors in England (p. 31).

Annette understands Jamaicans and criticises Mr Mason for his paternalistic attitude in regarding all black people as children (p. 28). She knows that there will be violence at their estate, but cannot convince her husband that she is right. When Coulibri is set on fire, she shows courage in risking her own life to save Pierre's (p. 33) and she would have risked it again, to go back for the parrot, Coco, but she was restrained.

When her son dies, she loses interest in her daughter, in her husband and in life generally. Mr Mason has her 'shut away' (p. 81) when she attacks him. For a while, he is lonely without her, but then 'he almost forgot her' (p. 110). She is guarded by a man and a woman who treat her roughly, and so she drinks to escape, and in the end 'she give up, she care for nothing' (p. 130). She dies, probably by committing suicide, when Antoinette is about sixteen (p. 51). As Antoinette tries to explain to Rochester: 'She did die when I was a child. There are always two deaths, the real one and the one people know about' (p. 106).

Antoinette's life parallels her mother's. Both marry in hope; both are left penniless; both are 'imprisoned' by husbands; both are accused of being lecherous, drunken and mad. Antoinette 'dies' when Rochester humiliates her with Amélie, just as Annette dies when Pierre is killed; their suicides are not so much a death as an escape from intolerable conditions.

Daniel Cosway/Boyd

Daniel Esau Cosway/Boyd is, from one point of view, the cause of the estrangement between Antoinette and her husband. He writes to Rochester, claiming to be Antoinette's illegitimate half-brother and sowing the seeds of discontent and fear in Rochester's mind.

It is not clear whether or not Daniel really is Antoinette's brother. Amélie is not certain (p. 99); Antoinette's father did not believe that Daniel was his son (p. 102); and Christophine insists that Daniel is a liar and no relative (p. 129). Whether related or not, however, he poisons Rochester's happiness and he does it with half-truths. He claims that Annette and her son were mad and suggests that Antoinette is 'going the same way' (p. 82); he stresses that Rochester is a stranger who cannot understand Creole ways; and he insinuates that Rochester was tricked into an unwise marriage and that everyone but Rochester knew how unwise it was.

Daniel Cosway is not simply an evil man, although he is mean, cruel and malicious. His words and actions bring misery to everyone with whom he is in contact. He is a self-righteous hypocrite, blaming everyone but himself for his poverty and problems. He is the only character in the novel who indulges in self-pity. Rochester is nauseated when Daniel tries to blackmail him (p. 104), but he allows the venom planted in his mind to poison his relationship with Antoinette.

All the characters in *Wide Sargasso Sea* suffer and some, like Daniel Cosway, cause others to suffer. Their pain is not seen, in a Christian light, as something which ennobles, but rather as an experience that can corrupt and destroy.

Grace Poole

In the final part of the novel, we meet the last narrator, Grace Poole. She is English and an employee of Rochester, who pays her '*double . . . the money*' (p. 145) she could expect for guarding his wife. We see Antoinette through her eyes as '*shivering and . . . so thin*' (p. 145) and as a '*girl who lives in her own darkness*' (p. 146). Although she assumes that Antoinette is mad, she cannot understand why Rochester does not treat her better in terms of food, hearing and clothing (p. 152).

Grace Poole is a working-class woman who uses a variety of English that is unique in the novel. She uses double negatives, such as '*I don't serve the devil for no money*' (p. 145) and refers to Mrs Fairfax as '*Mrs Eff*' (i.e. 'F'). Her narration is in italics both to distinguish it from the narratives of Antoinette and Rochester and to mark a transition from the West Indies to England.

Grace Poole accepts the job of looking after Antoinette because '*the world outside . . . can be a black and cruel world to a woman*' (p. 146). She drinks gin to keep her warm, to pass the time and also to blot out thoughts of the past. The gin makes her sleepy and allows Antoinette the opportunity to 'escape'.

The minor characters

There are a number of characters in *Wide Sargasso Sea* but each one makes a significant contribution to the plot. Mr Cosway is dead when the novel opens but we know quite a lot about him. His second wife, Annette, was very much younger than himself. He drank too much, was promiscuous and left his young wife and two children almost penniless when he died. He was, however, generous. All his illegitimate children were treated with kindness, and their mothers were given their freedom, a house and a piece of land (p. 101). He did not believe that Daniel was his son, but he provided for him, accepting that one extra child did not make much difference. As events reveal, this misjudgement has grave consequences for his daughter.

Aunt Cora is with the family when Coulibri is set on fire. Her courage and straight talking almost certainly saves them all (p. 37) because she knows and understands the local people in a way that Mr Mason never does. When Annette is ill Aunt Cora keeps Antoinette in Spanish Town and arranges for her to attend the convent, giving Antoinette the longest period of happiness in her life. She also spends several happy holidays with the family at Granbois (p. 68). Aunt Cora tries to persuade Richard Mason to safeguard Antoinette's financial future when her marriage is being arranged. Richard explains that he would trust Rochester with his life (p. 95) but is reminded by Aunt Cora that he is, in fact, entrusting Antoinette's life to Rochester. She worries about Rochester's character and refuses to go to their wedding. Many readers may wonder why Aunt Cora did not provide for Antoinette's financial future herself. We are never given the reason, but one point should be made. In English law, in the 1830s, unless a pre-nuptial arrangement was made to guarantee a woman's financial independence, all money belonging to her or left to her became the property of her husband. In other words, if Aunt Cora had left her money to Antoinette, it would have gone automatically to Rochester.

Sandi appears in all three parts of the novel. He saves Antoinette from some bullies on her first day at the convent (p. 42); he seems to have taught her to throw pebbles (p. 73) when she was a child; and he wants her to leave Rochester and go with him (pp. 151–2). He is described as Antoinette's 'cousin' (p. 42) but his father, Alexander, is her half brother (p. 103), thus making marriage between them impossible. Although he seems genuinely fond of Antoinette and concerned for her welfare, there is nothing he can do to intervene and protect her from Rochester's unwelcome attentions.

The nuns in the convent provide Antoinette with the refuge she needs at a crucial point in her life. She speaks of them with kindness and affection. Like Christophine, they were liberated women. They taught the girls to dance and when the bishop criticised their laxness, he was told to 'mind his own business' (p. 49).

Amélie is young, pretty and ambitious. She has little respect for 'white cockroaches', that is, the whites born in the Caribbean, but she is frightened of Christophine and unwilling to offend her. She is used by Rochester to hurt Antoinette and is then dismissed with a little money (p. 116). Amélie may have lost some dignity in sleeping with Rochester, but she feels in no way inferior to him. Indeed, she feels sorry for Rochester, and even sorrier for Antoinette.

Few of the characters in this novel are invariably attractive, because they are not romanticised. Jean Rhys is critical of people, rather than of either blacks or whites. She makes this point clear by using parallels. Tia might be seen as cruel for throwing a stone at Antoinette, but the two children are caught up in events that neither can control. They are both, in their own ways, victims: 'We stared at each other, blood on my face, tears on hers. It was as if I saw myself. Like in a looking-glass' (p. 38).

The least attractive character is the black man who looks after Annette. As Christophine explains to Rochester, 'he take her whenever he want', but even his cruelty is matched by Rochester's. Antoinette specifically draws a parallel between them, describing how she saw 'a black devil kissing her sad mouth. Like you kissed mine' (p. 121).

Jane Eyre and *Wide Sargasso Sea*

Similarities

(1) Both make use of a first-person narrative, which includes stream of consciousness (see 'Structure' pp. 42–4).
(2) Both heroines put considerable store by their dreams.
(3) Both suggest that Rochester is not entirely reliable. In *Jane Eyre* he is self-deceived about Jane's appearance (Chapter 24); calls £30,000 a pittance (Chapter 27); and claims that he could not be cruel even to Bertha, yet lodges her in a 'wild beast's den' (Chapter 27).
(4) Rochester's promiscuity is suggested. In *Wide Sargasso Sea*, he slept with Amélie. In *Jane Eyre*, he took three mistresses after incarcerating Bertha (Chapter 27).

Differences

(1) In *Jane Eyre*, Rochester claims that Bertha was five years older than him (Chapter 27); Antoinette is about five years younger than Rochester in *Wide Sargasso Sea*.
(2) In *Jane Eyre*, he claims that he was tricked into marrying 'Bertha' (Chapter 27) but when Antoinette wanted to call off the wedding, he persuaded her to change her mind.

The significance of the setting

Parts One and Two of the novel are set in the Caribbean, Part One in Jamaica and Part Two in the Windward Islands. England is the setting for Part Three only, and yet it, too, permeates the earlier sections, acting as a contrast to the West Indies.

Jamaica is described as an overgrown Eden. It is like the world perceived by Hamlet (*Hamlet*, Act I, Scene 2):

'Tis an unweeded garden
That grows to seed; things rank and gross in nature
Possess it merely.

Antoinette specifically draws attention to the similarity between Eden and the garden at Coulibri: 'Our garden was large and beautiful as that garden in the Bible – the tree of life grew there. But it had gone wild' (p. 16). The Windward Islands are equally beautiful, equally magical and yet, to Rochester, their beauty is cloying. Everything seems too bright, too colourful, too big. The islands have a vitality that is not shared by the main characters, all of whom, with the exception of Christophine, become zombie-like. Annette, Antoinette and, to some extent, Rochester, are neither wholly dead nor wholly alive. They share characteristics with the being described by Samuel Taylor Coleridge (1772–1832) in 'The Rime of the Ancient Mariner' (Pt III, v.11):

Her lips were red, *her* looks were free,
Her locks were yellow as gold:
Her skin was white as leprosy,
The Nightmare Life-in-Death was she,
Who thicks man's blood with cold.

The Caribbean is not anthropomorphised. Antoinette loves it because she has nothing else to love, but, as she reminds Rochester, it is 'as different as this God you call on so often' (p. 107).

England seems like a dream to Antoinette but as the only reality to Rochester. Her England is romantic, imaginary; put together from pictures and school books. Christophine's image of England is unromantic: 'I hear it cold to freeze your bones and they thief your money, clever like the devil. You have money in your pocket, you look again and bam! No money. Why you want to go to this cold thief place?' (p. 92).

England is the setting for Part Three, but it is an England that is confined to an upper room where 'you cannot see out' of the window (p. 147), where 'time has no meaning' (p. 151) and where Antoinette feels that she is 'dying because it is so cold and dark' (p. 150). If the Caribbean is bright and lush, the England of Thornfield Hall is dark, cold and sterile.

The time scheme

In this novel, Jean Rhys operates what might be described as a dual time scheme. We are never absolutely certain of the order of events, partly because they are not related in chronological sequence and partly because time is not seen as an absolute. Antoinette reminds Rochester that five years of poverty can be an eternity (p. 107) and she points out that time has 'no meaning' (p. 151) for a person in captivity, whether the captivity is mental or physical.

One possible time scheme is as follows:

- The Masons live in poverty for five years, while Antoinette is between the ages of about five and ten;
- Annette meets and marries Mr Mason and they are happy for perhaps three or four years;
- Coulibri is burnt down;
- Antoinette stays with her Aunt Cora for a few months;
- Antoinette goes to the convent between the ages of about fourteen to seventeen;
- Annette dies when Antoinette is sixteen;
- Antoinette is married at seventeen;
- The marriage is over within a few months;
- Antoinette is taken to England from Jamaica when she is still very young. (This would account for Grace Poole's description of her as a 'girl' (p. 146).)

Such a time scale would help explain why Rochester could behave so cruelly: he simply had no time to get to know his wife and he might have later assumed that Richard Mason had rushed the wedding so that he would not discover the problems in Antoinette's family.

An alternative time-scale suggests that considerably more time may have passed between events. We are never told how or when Antoinette became so friendly with Sandi that there should be talk that they would get married, but there is certainly tenderness between them (pp. 151–2). We do not know when the family went to Granbois. Antoinette tells Rochester that they 'used to come here . . . in June, July and August' (p. 68) and that she had visited it three times with Aunt Cora, explaining 'That was after . . .' (p. 68) but never saying after what. It might have been the death of her mother, but then Antoinette would have been at least twenty when she married Rochester. Ultimately, temporal preciseness is unimportant in the novel. What matters is how people treat each other.

Concluding remarks

Wide Sargasso Sea is a novel of alienation, a novel of struggle and oppositions: between women and men, black and white, rich and poor, free and enslaved, sanity and madness, warm and cold, love and hate, good and evil. It is, however, a mark of the novel's subtlety that such dichotomies are established and then challenged. Antoinette, for example, is 'free' but enslaved by Rochester and a patriarchal legal system; she is white, but receives love and understanding from Christophine, who is black, and from Sandi, who is half black; she becomes 'mad' to escape an insane world; and she escapes a living death by dying.

Wide Sargasso Sea may seem like a Gothic novel. It is not one, although it has many of the characteristics associated with this genre. It establishes an atmosphere of gloom in which the grotesque and the supernatural become the norm. Yet *Wide Sargasso Sea* is much more than a Gothic narrative. It is a poetic exploration of aspects of the human condition, especially love and sexual power, death and the loss of identity.

Part 4

Hints for study

Studying *Wide Sargasso Sea*

Novels, as their name suggests, are a comparatively modern genre, dating back no earlier than the late sixteenth century. Whereas poetry and drama are most fully appreciated when spoken aloud, the novel is usually read in silence. Like drama, it can tell a story, often involving many characters and the passage of time, but its uniqueness lies in the way we, as readers, can enter the minds of the main characters.

Understanding a novel is based on three stages: reading and responding; checking your response; evaluating. Often, when we read a novel, we are not absolutely certain of the writer's intentions. We can, of course, clearly perceive the main events in the story. We can recognise strongly held opinions on sexual love, perhaps, or on the relative positions of women and men in society. We can also react to aspects of the novel on an emotional level, before we respond to them intellectually. The word 'nothing', for example, is used and re-used in every section of *Wide Sargasso Sea*, unobtrusively influencing our reaction and reinforcing a sense of sadness, depression and hopelessness.

When we have noted our response, we should check to see if we can support or refine it. If we have sensed melancholy, for example, is it because of the story, or because of our identification with a particular character, or because of the words and imagery used? Or is it, indeed, a fusion of all three? Are the sentences disjointed, reflecting disjointed thoughts? Are there any images that can help to explain our reaction? Do we identify more readily with Antoinette than with Rochester because she is so often associated with bright colours? Do we link Antoinette with the parrot, Coco? It, too, is brightly coloured. It, too, is imprisoned. It, too, asks questions that nobody answers. And it, too, dies in a fire. Do we, in fact, feel that the novel's outcome is inevitable because we have, at some level, noticed the repeated images, the repeated events, the repeated mistakes? Gradually, by thinking about characters and incidents and by re-reading the novel, we deepen our understanding.

By this stage, we have begun to evaluate the novel, assessing how effectively the writer controls story, characters, words and images and, through them, our response. The evaluation should not be either mechanical or superficial. It should always be based on our own reactions, reactions which have been informed by a close reading of the text.

Secondly, we should remember that, in our comments, we are offering an interpretation of a novel, and that an interpretation is always partial, never complete. That explains why two people can respond strongly, yet differently, to the same work. It is perfectly feasible that one reader will regard Antoinette as a victim of male oppression, whereas another will see that Rochester, too, is a victim. Like Antoinette, he was rejected by a parent and, like Shakespeare's Othello, he finds himself in an alien country, surrounded by people whom he cannot fully understand. As long as we can support our point of view by reference to the text, our evaluation will be valid.

Topics for discussion

When we first read *Wide Sargasso Sea*, it may seem simple and straightforward. A closer reading, however, reveals that the simplicity is the result of consummate artistry, rather than of spontaneity. No detail is provided without a reason. As early as p. 18, for example, we are told that Christophine was the only woman in Jamaica to wear her headtie with 'two high points in front'. This simple detail underlines Christophine's uniqueness. She is the only character in the novel who is not constrained by the opinion of others.

Similar points may be made about every character and, indeed, every action. Initially, we may despise Rochester's cruelty. A close reading of the text, however, makes us realise that, in depriving Antoinette of joy, he has also ensured his own unhappiness. He destroyed Antoinette out of fear rather than inhumanity. He was afraid to trust his instincts, afraid of losing control. Rochester is not just an evil Bluebeard who keeps his wife in the attic. He is also a Heathcliff character who loses the woman who might have humanised him.

Jean Rhys's greatest achievement in this novel is that she leaves room for doubt and discussion. Your appreciation of the novel will be deepened if you discuss some, or all, of the following topics:

(1) Madness is one of the themes of the novel. How would you describe madness? Does your definition overlap Jean Rhys's? Was Annette mad? Was Antoinette mad? Always? Did she become mad? Was she driven mad? Was madness an escape from an unbearable reality? Was Rochester mad? Is cruelty a form of madness? Can the term madness be used to condone unacceptable behaviour? Does Jean Rhys question conventional ideas of madness? How?

(2) What is Jean Rhys's attitude to slavery? Does it apply only to people of Afro-Caribbean origin or could other people be bought and sold? Does slavery corrupt? (Contrast the behaviour of Annette's carers with that of Baptiste and the cook on p. 117, for example. Consider also Christophine's courage and loyalty.)

(3) Describe and discuss Jean Rhys's attitude to the natural world. Does she suggest that the natural environment plays a role in forming our characters? Does she suggest that our view of nature is conditioned by our characters? Why did the Caribbean seem 'wild' and 'beautiful' to Antoinette but 'alien' to Rochester? Does Rhys use nature as a metaphor for human relationships? How? Discuss the thematic significance of the Sargasso Sea in the novel.

(4) Many novels that deal with childhood are described as sentimental. How does Jean Rhys avoid sentimentality in her creation of Antoinette's childhood? What is the significance of the childhood relationships between Antoinette and Tia and between Antoinette and the girls in her convent school?

(5) Rejection of a child by a parent is a theme in *Wide Sargasso Sea*. Antoinette is rejected by her mother, by Tia and by Rochester; Rochester is rejected by his father and his elder brother; Daniel Cosway is rejected by his father and Antoinette. Describe how these rejections have influenced the characters of Antoinette, Rochester and Daniel. Is it significant that one of the most attractive characters, Sandi, is loved by his father?

(6) Examine the proportions of the novel. Is it significant that the three parts are so asymmetrical? (Part One is just over 27 per cent, Part Two is over 64 per cent and Part Three is less than 9 per cent. Less than 42 per cent of the narrative is in Antoinette's words; almost 58 per cent of the story is told in Rochester's words.) Given the fact that most of the narrative is recorded in Rochester's voice, why does he not engage more of our sympathy?

(7) Is *Wide Sargasso Sea* a Gothic novel? (A Gothic novel is sometimes defined as one which is characterised by gloom, the grotesque and the supernatural. Such novels were popular in the eighteenth century.) If you believe that it is a Gothic novel, do you think that such a classification is a criticism? If you think it is not a Gothic novel, how is it saved from being classified as such? (Does the brevity of the novel have any bearing on this topic?)

(8) Many people have claimed that *Jane Eyre* is a novel that appeals mainly to female readers. Do you think that the same generalisation can be applied to *Wide Sargasso Sea*? If you do, do you think this is a weakness? If you think that *Wide Sargasso Sea* appeals also and/or equally to male readers, explain why this is so.

(9) Most novelists have avoided using non-standard English for any of the main characters in their novels. Why? Is correctness of speech, in some way, associated with moral rectitude? Jean Rhys uses not only patois but also creole English for Christophine. Why? What advantages of characterisation did she gain in using a creole? Discuss the view that, in *Wide Sargasso Sea*, the creole is the voice of both

truth and kindness. Are there any endearments in English? Do you think many readers miss the significance of such terms of affection as *Doudou ché*? Could this be a weakness? Could it allow a reader to undervalue the love between Christophine and Antoinette?

(10) Has *Wide Sargasso Sea* caused you to think in a new way about such subjects as madness, rejection, slavery, male-female relationships? If so, do you think of this as a mark of a great novel? Should a novel make us think about such subjects? Would they be better treated in a social tract? Is 'better' the same as 'more memorable'?

How to write about *Wide Sargasso Sea*

Each of us, with practice, evolves our own style. In writing about literature, however, it may be useful to employ a number of strategies. These are meant as a support for your ideas, not as a substitute for them.

Having read the novel, thought about it, and discussed your views, you may feel that it is helpful to write about some or all of its constituents. With a novel, it is usually helpful to consider the story, the characters, the setting, the structure and the imagery.

First, let us take the level of story. Briefly, *Wide Sargasso Sea* deals with love and betrayal, with misunderstanding and cruelty. At one level, it describes the meeting and marriage of a seventeen-year-old Jamaican girl and a young Englishman, their initial attraction for each other, his rejection of her when he 'discovers' insanity in her family, their estrangement, his incarceration of her in his English manor, and her eventual escape through suicide. At another level, however, it represents the lack of understanding between men and women, black and white, rich and poor, and it challenges the belief that, through suffering, a person may be purified or ennobled. In *Wide Sargasso Sea*, suffering corrupts and destroys.

Secondly, we should examine the characters. We can do this mainly by examining their actions, by what they say about themselves and what others say about them. Often, in a novel, the voice of the narrator can provide information which we know to be true. Jane Austen's *Emma* (1815), for example, opens with certain facts about the heroine:

> Emma Woodhouse, handsome, clever, and rich, with a comfortable home and happy disposition, seemed to unite some of the best blessings of existence; and had lived nearly twenty-one years in the world with very little to distress or vex her.

Wide Sargasso Sea is different. There is no objective authorial voice and therefore no absolute truth. All our information is provided through either Antoinette, Rochester or Grace Poole and so we always get a view of the truth rather than absolute certainty. We do not know, for example, whether or not Daniel is Antoinette's half brother. His rejection by his white family might, in part, account for his cruel betrayal of Antoinette. Rochester assumes the relationship but Christophine suggests otherwise. We might also query the suggestion that Rochester needed Antoinette's dowry. In the first paragraph of Part Three, however, Grace Poole claims that 'he was a wealthy man' before the death of his father and brother. Because there is no authorial voice providing us with facts, we must evaluate all the information we get, sifting suggestion from opinion, belief from supposition.

Thirdly, we should think of the settings of the novel and, in particular, of the contrast between the warmth, colour and freedom of Jamaica and the cold, grey restrictiveness of Thornfield Hall. Antoinette is identified with Jamaica, with its lushness and unpredictability. Rochester, for a while, is in love with both, but he rejects their extravagance: 'Everything is too much ... Too much blue, too much purple, too much green' (p. 59). He might well have added 'too much mystery, too much feeling'.

Fourthly, it may be of value to consider the structure of the novel. Is it written in the first person, using 'I' or in the third person, using 'he' or 'she' or 'they'? Is it written in the present tense or in the past? Is the style formal or colloquial or casual? Does the novelist use direct or reported speech? Is the language aimed at a young reader? an older reader? at women? at men? at a wide audience? Are we told what to think or are we allowed to make up our own minds? Why are there no chapters in *Wide Sargasso Sea*? Would they give an impression of regularity and discreteness that would conflict with Jean Rhys's intention to involve the readers fully in the story, absorbing their interest in its entirety rather than in segments? To see how even subtle structural changes can affect a reader, let us consider how the last paragraph in Part Two might have been written. We might have had:

The young boy followed them, unthinking, the basket balanced on his head. He used the back of his hand to wipe away his tears. Who would have thought that any boy would cry like that for nothing?

or:

The young boy follows them, unthinking, the basket balanced on his head. He uses the back of his hand to wipe away his tears. Who would think that any boy would cry like this for nothing?

or:

The stupid young man followed them, his basket balanced on his head. Using the back of his hand he wiped away his tears. It would have been difficult to imagine that any one would cry in such a manner for nothing.

or:

The young boy follows us, stupidly, with a basket balanced on his head. 'What are you crying for? Don't use the back of your hand to dry your eyes. Who on earth would have thought that you would cry like that for nothing?'

Now compare these versions with the original:

> That stupid boy followed us, the basket balanced on his head. He used the back of his hand to wipe away his tears. Who would have thought that any boy would cry like that. For nothing. Nothing . . .

The changes we have made are small but they affect the relationship established between the writer and the reader. They do not just say the same things in different ways. Each says something different. Every word, every structure, everything told and everything omitted is of significance in a great work of literature.

In examining the structures used by a novelist, we might also ask if she uses short or long sentences, statements, questions, exclamations or negatives. Such structures covertly influence our responses. We might also look at the words used and whether or not they belong to a particular register, such as love, nature or religion. The subject matter influences the choice of words. The final section of Part One, for example, deals with the convent where Antoinette has found peace and some understanding and we find many words which reinforce this feeling, words such as 'refuge', 'place of sunshine', 'serene', 'gold sunlight', 'happiness', 'modesty', 'perpetual light', 'soul', 'loved', 'brightness', 'light', 'sun', 'ecstasy'. But, almost like a counterpoint, other words creep in, emphasising the uncertainty of life outside the convent, 'death', 'shadows', a repeated phrase from the prayer the Hail Mary 'now and at the hour of our death', 'body', 'hated', 'dark', 'perish'.

Finally, we should be aware that a writer's imagery can influence us, even before we fully understand how or why. When we think that a novel is gentle or violent, angry or composed, contemporary or old-fashioned, we are often responding to the writer's use of imagery. *Wide Sargasso Sea* has recurrent inter-related images of light, dark, religion, life, death, nature and colours. They are associated with people and their moods, and with places and their associations. Antoinette's peace of mind is linked to the light. As she tells Rochester: 'I was always happy in the morning, not always in the afternoon, and never after sunset' (p. 109). Her punishment in being incarcerated in a room with a window that she cannot see out of (p. 147) is double torment in that she has lost both freedom and light.

It is perhaps worth pointing out, in connection with the above quotation, how often Jean Rhys uses triads, groups of words or phrases in threes, as an expression of strong feelings:

> always happy in the morning
> not always in the afternoon
> never after sunset

Similar triads occur, for example, when Rochester first indicates his attraction to Amélie who appears 'so full of delighted malice, so intelligent . . . so intimate' (p. 57) and, perhaps most poignantly of all when Antoinette describes her goodbye to Sandi: 'The white ship whistled three times, once gaily, once calling, once to say goodbye' (p. 152).

Antoinette is frequently described in terms of flowers which are fragile and as easily destroyed as the frangipani wreath Rochester crushes with his foot on their honeymoon night (p. 62). Rochester, on the other hand, is described in terms of more permanent images, suggesting that he is less easily influenced. Antoinette makes this point overtly when she tells him: 'That's how you are. A stone' (p. 122).

Answering questions on *Wide Sargasso Sea*

There is no set of mechanical rules which we can follow in preparing to answer questions on any writer. The most useful piece of advice is to know the texts. Read them; think about them; talk about them; try to understand them. When it comes to answering essay questions or examination topics, it is advisable to keep the following points in mind:

(1) Read the question carefully, ensuring that you know exactly what is required of you.
(2) Plan your answer in points before writing your essay. A good essay will have an introductory paragraph devoted to a consideration of the topic, separate paragraphs on each of the points you make, and a concluding paragraph evaluating the topic from your point of view.
(3) Use quotations, even one- or two-word quotations, in support of your opinion. There is, of course, no need to quote the page reference in an examination although it may be a useful scholarly exercise in project work. Page references are supplied in these notes to help you find the quotations easily.
(4) Write simply, clearly and honestly. There is no particular merit in long sentences and polysyllabic words. Examiners are interested in your views on *Wide Sargasso Sea*, rather than on those of teachers or critics.
(5) Always re-read your essays. If you cannot understand what you have written, no-one else will.

Specimen questions and suggested answer patterns

It is neither useful nor desirable to offer students a set of 'model' answers, since over-reliance on such answers can limit original thinking and discourage students from using their own knowledge creatively. These Notes are intended to train minds, not memories. Nevertheless, it may be helpful to indicate how a student might deal with a topic, and so one full sample essay is provided, together with two essay plans. If you disagree with some of the points made, that is good, but notice that the subject is dealt with logically and systematically.

Question 1: 'It is impossible to appreciate *Wide Sargasso Sea* fully without having detailed knowledge of *Jane Eyre*.' Discuss.

Plan

INTRODUCTION:

What is meant by 'appreciate fully'?
Can we appreciate the story only in part if we have not read *Jane Eyre*?
Can we appreciate *Wide Sargasso Sea* more, although differently, without having read *Jane Eyre*?
Is it perhaps a criticism of *Wide Sargasso Sea* to suggest that it is in some way incomplete?

BODY OF ESSAY:

It is certainly easier to understand the novel, on first reading, if we are aware of its relationship to *Jane Eyre*.
It is also possible to respond to the power and poetry of the novel even if we have never heard of *Jane Eyre*.
If *Wide Sargasso Sea* depended on *Jane Eyre*, then it would be an incomplete novel. But this is not true.

CONCLUSION:

Wide Sargasso Sea can be appreciated without our having read *Jane Eyre*. There are even positive reasons why we should read it in and for itself without reference to another novel. Rhys's great achievement is that she 'justifies' the mad Creole woman. Anyone who reads *Wide Sargasso Sea* automatically reinterprets *Jane Eyre*.

Essay Answer:

Every reader of a novel will take individual strengths to it. If we know a great deal about the history of the French Revolution, for example, we may find that we respond more fully to *A Tale of Two Cities* by Charles Dickens. If we have read or heard about the social conditions for poor blacks in the United States, we may have a fuller understanding of the conflicts in Alice Walker's *The Color Purple*. All our knowledge, experience and sensitivity will contribute something to our appreciation of *Wide Sargasso Sea*. If part of that knowledge is a familiarity with *Jane Eyre*, then we will notice how Jean Rhys manipulates the characters and events in *Jane Eyre* to suit her creative purposes. We will thus bring an extra dimension of sensitivity and awareness to our reading of Jean Rhys's novel. We will also, perhaps, bring prejudices, in that our opinions of

Rochester and Antoinette, in particular, will inevitably be affected by our memories of *Jane Eyre*. Our reading of all novels will, to some extent, benefit from knowledge which we have acquired elsewhere. To claim, however, that we can only 'fully' appreciate *Wide Sargasso Sea* if we know Charlotte Brontë's novel is to underestimate the skill and talent of Jean Rhys. The response to Rhys's novel will be different, but no less profound, if we are unfamiliar with the Brontë tale which was its inspiration.

From the very first page of *Wide Sargasso Sea*, we are allowed to hear the thoughts and experiences of a young white girl, growing up in poverty in the Caribbean during the nineteenth century. The background information is provided subtly but unequivocally as we hear about Jamaica, the Emancipation Act, the decaying estates and the solitary nature of the child narrator. Gradually, the story of Antoinette unfolds. We learn of her attachment to a former slave, called Christophine; we become aware of her mother's depression because her son, Pierre, is handicapped; we see an improvement in the family's finances when her mother marries a rich widower; and we are prepared for the difficulties that arise in the marriage arranged between Antoinette and a young stranger from England.

Jean Rhys never names this young Englishman. We see him through the eyes of Antoinette and we hear his own account of his emotional turmoil when he learns that Antoinette's mother was a drunkard who committed suicide, that her brother was an 'imbecile' and that his wife is thought to be showing early signs of the madness that has developed on both sides of her family. Because Antoinette's husband is never named, he always remains distant, mysterious, perhaps even dangerous. Whatever name we use for him emphasises an aspect of his life or of a relationship, without actually personalising him. We could call him 'the man', 'the English-man', 'the stranger', 'Antoinette's husband', 'an adventurer', or perhaps simply 'he', but each choice, in part, conditions our response to his character. It is certainly easier to think of him as Rochester, the name of Charlotte Brontë's hero but, in giving him a name, we humanise him.

If we have read *Jane Eyre* before reading *Wide Sargasso Sea*, we know that Antoinette is doomed. Her death has been pre-ordained by Brontë. Such knowledge allows us to respond to Coco's death, for example, not just as the death of a parrot, but as a prefiguring of Antoinette's suicide. It also adds a fatalistic dimension to the novel. No matter how hard Antoinette struggles to establish a relationship with her husband, no matter how much advice and support she gets from Christophine, her fate is sealed. She is condemned to become the 'mad Creole woman' who haunts Thornfield Hall.

Wide Sargasso Sea is a novel of considerable power. Its style is poetic and its characterisation vivid. It may owe its origins to *Jane Eyre* and it may certainly be easier to understand if we have read the earlier novel. It is, however, a great, tragic novel in its own right. It examines human interaction, explores human misunderstandings and evokes a cathartic response in its readers whether or not they have read *Jane Eyre*.

Wide Sargasso Sea can be appreciated without our having a knowledge of *Jane Eyre*. There are many reasons why we should read it in and for itself without reference to another novel. Rhys's great achievement, however, is that she 'justifies' the mad Creole woman. No-one who reads *Wide Sargasso Sea* will ever be able to dismiss her as conveniently as Charlotte Brontë does. One could go further, indeed, and claim that *Jane Eyre* can only be fully appreciated by someone who has read *Wide Sargasso Sea*.

Question 2: Write a detailed analysis of Antoinette's character, indicating if and why you find her an attractive and appealing heroine.

Plan
For this type of essay, you should remember that an evaluation of any character depends on an analysis of what the character says, what she does and what other people say about her.

INTRODUCTION:
Comment briefly on Antoinette's life from the poverty and freedom of Coulibri, through the hopeful phase of her marriage, to the pain and privation of a life without light, warmth or colour.

BODY OF ESSAY:
What do Antoinette's words reveal about herself? Is she caring? Does she consider the needs of other people? Is she thoughtful? Is she brave? Has she got a sense of humour? Is she arrogant? In Part One, is there criticism of anyone? Of the mother who rejected her? Of Tia, the friend who finds herself in the opposing camp? Of Mr Mason, who puts her mother away and then forgets about her?

In Part Two, Antoinette criticises Amélie, her husband and Daniel Cosway. Are her criticisms justified? In Part Three, do her words reveal anger and bitterness or resignation and a desire to escape? What do Antoinette's actions reveal about her? She tries to please Mr Mason; she fits happily into the life at school; she treats her black 'cousins' with kindness; she tries to rescue her mother; she tries to win back her husband's affection; she tries to follow Christophine's advice to tell her husband the truth; she speaks up for the boy who is being left behind by her husband; she shows patience and intelligence in arranging to set fire to Thornfield Hall.

What do other people say or think about her? Christophine loves her and tries to protect her. She does not want even her own son to see Antoinette in such a depressed condition; Sandi loves her and would save her if he could; Grace Poole feels sorry that she has such poor clothes and food; her husband learns to despise her, but only, perhaps, because he despises himself; Daniel hates her, but he hates almost everyone; Amélie hurts her but feels sorry for her too.

CONCLUSION:
Antoinette is a complex but attractive character. She endures her hardships with courage and determination.

Question 3: *Wide Sargasso Sea* has been described as a 'feminist novel'. Say what you think is implied by this description and indicate whether or not you agree with it.

Plan

Remember that there are three parts to this question. You must define what is meant by a feminist novel; say whether and in what ways *Wide Sargasso Sea* could be characterised as a feminist novel; and evaluate whether or not such a label is appropriate.

INTRODUCTION:
A feminist novel is one which may do some or all of the following:
Concentrate on female issues, characters and interests; expose the injustice in patriarchal views, customs and laws; and stress gender-based inequalities and argue (either overtly or covertly) for an equivalisation of roles. *Wide Sargasso Sea* can be seen to fulfil some of these criteria.

BODY OF ESSAY:
Wide Sargasso Sea deals, primarily, with the thoughts and actions of Antoinette, even though her husband controls a greater proportion of the narrative.
It is concerned with love, marriage, instability, deceit, treachery and tragedy.
It exposes the inequalities in society, inequalities involving black and white as well as male and female.
It can, therefore, be seen to reflect feminist issues.
On the other hand, it indicates that both Rochester and Antoinette are trapped; it shows that human beings are a complex mixture of good and bad, strength and weakness; the men are not all unattractive any more than the women are all attractive. It might be useful, for your own purposes, to draw a chart, showing where you would place the main characters:

Attractive	*Mixed*	*Unattractive*
Antoinette	Mr Mason	Daniel
Christophine	?Aunt Cora	?Rochester
Sandi	Annette	?Amélie

CONCLUSION

To classify any piece of literature as a 'social' novel or a 'feminist' novel or a 'Gothic' novel is to reduce it by suggesting that it fits perfectly into a narrow category. A great novel will reflect the issues and preoccupations of both its writer and its age, but it will also transcend them. In *Wide Sargasso Sea*, Jean Rhys tackles topics that have been raised by feminists, but she tackles them as an illustration of 'man's inhumanity to man' (Robert Burns, 'Man Was Made to Mourn') and, in this context, 'man' includes 'woman'.

Revision questions

Questions dealing with general aspects of the novel

The following questions should help you in your work on *Wide Sargasso Sea*.

(1) *Wide Sargasso Sea* poses the question 'Why do such terrible things occur in life?' Does Jean Rhys provide the reader with any answers to this question?

(2) Describe and discuss Jean Rhys's major skills as a novelist.

(3) Jean Rhys writes about suffering and alienation. Does this mean we can classify her as a 'depressing' writer? Support your answer by close reference to *Wide Sargasso Sea*.

(4) 'Part of the power of *Wide Sargasso Sea* comes from the use of echoes. Antoinette's fate repeats her mother's; Rochester's cruelty is a reminder of Mr Mason's indifference.' Do you agree with this statement? Support your answer by close analysis of the novel.

(5) Illustrate and discuss Rhys's views on love and friendship in the novel.

(6) 'Although Antoinette and Rochester seem very different, in both cases their actions stem from the insecurity caused by being rejected by a parent.' Discuss.

(7) Examine Rhys's preoccupation with one or more of the following motifs: the injustice of slavery; the relationship between men and women; the fear of the unknown; the influence of one's surroundings on one's behaviour.

(8) 'Rochester is not a tragic hero. To be a tragic hero, one may have a flaw, but the flaw must not be such an ignoble flaw as cruelty.' Discuss.

(9) What is the purpose of the many literary, cultural and religious allusions in Rhys's novel?

(10) 'By changing the narrative voices, Jean Rhys provides her readers with different perspectives. She also puts readers in the position that their opinion is not merely optional. It is essential. In a very real

sense, all readers of *Wide Sargasso Sea* create their own version of the novel.' Do you agree with this claim?

Questions dealing with specific points in the novel

(1) Explain the role of Daniel Cosway in *Wide Sargasso Sea*.

(2) Compare the characters of Tia and Amélie. Did they betray Antoinette or was their behaviour conditioned by the circumstances in which they found themselves. (Do not forget the 'appearance' of Tia in Part Three.)

(3) Give an account of Antoinette's behaviour to her servants. Did she win their loyalty?

(4) Describe and discuss the relationship between Antoinette and Christophine.

(5) 'Annette was not mad but events made her mad.' Discuss.

(6) 'Antoinette and Rochester are as different as the landscapes of their childhoods.' What validity is there in such a claim?

(7) Approximately 60 per cent of the narrative is given to Rochester. Much of what happens, therefore, is told by him. What devices are used by Rhys to ensure that our sympathies stay with Antoinette?

(8) Discuss the value of using creolised English in *Wide Sargasso Sea*.

(9) What part is played in the development of the plot by the following characters: Mr Mason, Richard Mason, Aunt Cora, Amélie and Sandi?

(10) 'Christophine is the heroine of *Wide Sargasso Sea*.' Discuss.

Part 5

Suggestions for further reading

The text

RHYS, JEAN: *Wide Sargasso Sea*, Penguin, Harmondsworth, 1968.

Works by Jean Rhys

The Left Bank and Other Stories, Jonathan Cape, London, 1927; reprinted Books for Libraries Press, New York, 1970.
Postures, Chatto & Windus, London, 1928; published as *Quartet*, Simon & Schuster, New York, 1929; reprinted André Deutsch, 1969.
After Leaving Mr Mackenzie, Jonathan Cape, London, 1931.
Voyage in the Dark, Constable, London, 1939.
Good Morning, Midnight, Constable, London, 1939.
Wide Sargasso Sea, W. W. Norton, New York, 1966.
Tigers Are Better Looking, André Deutsch, London, 1968; paperback edition, Penguin Books, Harmondsworth, 1972.
My Day: Three Pieces by Jean Rhys, Frank Hallman, New York, 1975.
Sleep It Off, Lady, Harper & Row, New York, 1976.
Smile Please: An Unfinished Autobiography, André Deutsch, London, 1979.
WYNDHAM, FRANCIS and MELLY, DIANA (EDS): *Jean Rhys Letters, 1931–1966*, André Deutsch, London, 1984.
Jean Rhys: The Early Novels, André Deutsch, London, 1984.
Jean Rhys: The Complete Novels, W. W. Norton, New York, 1985.
Jean Rhys: The Collected Short Stories, W. W. Norton, New York, 1987.

Selected reviews of *Wide Sargasso Sea*

ALLEN, WALTER: 'Bertha the Doomed', *New York Times Book Review*, 18 June, 1966, p. 5.
BRAYBROOKE, NEVILLE: *Spectator*, 28 October, 1966, p. 560.
COOK, HILLARY: *Listener*, 19 January, 1967, p. 103.
HEARNE, JOHN: *Cornhill*, Summer 1974, pp. 323–33.
HOPE, FRANCIS: 'The First Mrs. Rochester', *New Statesman*, 28 October, 1966, p. 638.
KERSH, GERALD: *Saturday Review of Literature*, 1 July, 1967, p. 23.

Biographical and critical studies

ANGIER, CAROLE: *Jean Rhys: Life and Works*, André Deutsch, London, 1990.

DAVIDSON, A. K.: *Jean Rhys*, Frederick Ungar, New York, 1985.

HOWELLS, CORAL ANN: *Jean Rhys*, Harvester Wheatsheaf, Brighton, 1991.

JAMES, LOUIS: *Jean Rhys*, Longman, London, 1978.

JAMES, SELMA: *The Ladies and the Mammies: Jane Austen and Jean Rhys*, Falling Wall Press, 1983.

MELLOWN, E. W.: *Jean Rhys: A Descriptive and Annotated Bibliography of Works and Criticism*, Garland Publishing Inc., New York and London, 1984.

NEBEKER, HELEN: *Jean Rhys: Woman in Passage*, Eden Press, Montreal, 1981.

O'CONNOR, TERESA: *Jean Rhys: The West Indian Novels*, New York University Press, New York and London, 1986.

PLANTE, DAVID: *Difficult Women*, Gollancz, London, 1983.

STALEY, THOMAS F.: *Jean Rhys: A Critical Study*, University of Texas Press, Austin, 1979.

VREELAND, ELIZABETH: 'Jean Rhys', *Paris Review*, 21, Fall 1979, pp. 219–37.

WOLFE, PETER: *Jean Rhys*, Twayne Publishers, Boston, 1980.

WYNDHAM, FRANCIS: 'Introduction to Jean Rhys', *London Magazine*, January, 1960, pp. 15–18.

Background to the West Indies

ATWOOD, THOMAS: *The History of the Island of Dominica*, Frank Cass, London, 1971.

BRAITHWAITE, EDWARD: *The Development of Creole Society in Jamaica, 1770–1820*, Clarendon Press, Oxford, 1971.

CASSIDY, F. G.: *Jamaica Talk: Three Hundred Years of the English Language in Jamaica*, Macmillan, London, 1961.

DAVY, JOHN: *The West Indies, Before and Since Slave Emancipation*, W. and G. Cash, London, 1854.

EDWARDS, BRYAN: *The History, Civil and Commercial, of the British Colonies of the West Indies*, Stockdale, London, 1807.

HOYT, E. P.: *African Slavery*, Abelard-Schuman, London, 1973.

NUNN, H. P. V. (ED.): *Lady Nugent's Journal of her Residence in Jamaica from 1801 to 1805*, Blackwell, Oxford, 1966.

TODD, LORETO: *Pidgins and Creoles*, Routledge, London, 1990.

The author of these notes

LORETO TODD is Reader in International English at the University of Leeds. Educated in Northern Ireland and England, she has degrees in English Language, Literature and Linguistics. Dr Todd has taught in England and in West Africa, and has lectured in Australia, Canada, the Caribbean, Europe, Papua New Guinea, Singapore and the United States of America. She has published twenty books, including *International English Usage* (1990), *Variety in Contemporary English* (1991) and *York Notes on Derek Walcott* (1993). At present, she is compiling an Audio-Visual Archive of International English.